1983

The Abortion Dispute
and the American System

Gilbert Y. Steiner, Editor

The Abortion Dispute
and the American System

LAWRENCE M. FRIEDMAN

ROGER H. DAVIDSON

G. CALVIN MACKENZIE

JOHN E. JACKSON *and* MARIS A. VINOVSKIS

CYNTHIA E. HARRISON

THE BROOKINGS INSTITUTION
Washington, D.C.

Library of Congress Cataloging in Publication data:

Main entry under title:

The Abortion dispute and the American system.

Includes bibliographical references.

1. Abortion—Government policy—United States—
Congresses. 2. Abortion—United States—Moral and
ethical aspects—Congresses. 3. Abortion—Law and
legislation—United States—Congresses. I. Steiner,
Gilbert Yale, 1924–   . II. Brookings Institution.
HQ767.5.U5A24   1983   363.4'6'0973   82-45978
ISBN 0-8157-8125-3

1 2 3 4 5 6 7 8 9

THE BROOKINGS INSTITUTION is an independent organization devoted to nonpartisan research, education, and publication in economics, government, foreign policy, and the social sciences generally. Its principal purposes are to aid in the development of sound public policies and to promote public understanding of issues of national importance.

The Institution was founded on December 8, 1927, to merge the activities of the Institute for Government Research, founded in 1916, the Institute of Economics, founded in 1922, and the Robert Brookings Graduate School of Economics and Government, founded in 1924.

The Board of Trustees is responsible for the general administration of the Institution, while the immediate direction of the policies, program, and staff is vested in the President, assisted by an advisory committee of the officers and staff. The by-laws of the Institution state: "It is the function of the Trustees to make possible the conduct of scientific research, and publication, under the most favorable conditions, and to safeguard the independence of the research staff in the pursuit of their studies and in the publication of the results of such studies. It is not a part of their function to determine, control, or influence the conduct of particular investigations or the conclusions reached."

The President bears final responsibility for the decision to publish a manuscript as a Brookings book. In reaching his judgment on the competence, accuracy, and objectivity of each study, the President is advised by the director of the appropriate research program and weighs the views of a panel of expert outside readers who report to him in confidence on the quality of the work. Publication of a work signifies that it is deemed a competent treatment worthy of public consideration but does not imply endorsement of conclusions or recommendations.

The Institution maintains its position of neutrality on issues of public policy in order to safeguard the intellectual freedom of the staff. Hence interpretations or conclusions in Brookings publications should be understood to be solely those of the authors and should not be attributed to the Institution, to its trustees, officers, or other staff members, or to the organizations that support its research.

Foreword

ABORTION POLICY as a public question has produced unyielding positions at either extreme and ambivalence in the middle. The United States is far from any consensus on the ethical and theological issues involved in this complex and depressing problem. But since the Supreme Court's 1973 decision in *Roe* v. *Wade*, national abortion policy has been explicit, as have efforts to change it by several states and localities. The seemingly unending and fierce battle over abortion policy is either fought or reflected in each branch of the national government as well as in electoral campaigns.

This volume evaluates how that battle affects the governmental system. It begins with four essays appraising the influence on governmental and political institutions of the means employed to achieve either pro-life or pro-choice policy ends. It then summarizes the reactions to those appraisals by public affairs experts and activist leaders on both sides of the abortion dispute who accepted Brookings' invitation to participate in a day-long symposium on the subject.

The inquiry and the plan for carrying it out were framed by Gilbert Y. Steiner, a senior fellow in the Brookings Governmental Studies program. Martha Derthick, director of the Governmental Studies program, and Professor Robert Mnookin of Stanford Law School commented helpfully on various parts of the manuscript. Diane Hodges furnished administrative support. Both Nancy D. Davidson, who edited the manuscript, and Joan P. Milan, who processed it for publication, provided thoughtful assistance at numerous stages. They, Robert A. Katzmann, Margaret A. Latus, and Cynthia E. Harrison each made available extensive notes on the symposium discussion.

The Institution is grateful for the interest of the participants in the symposium. They were not asked to review Steiner's account of the reactions of the symposium, however, and no participant necessarily agrees with the conclusions stated there.

Oscar Harkavy of the Ford Foundation emphasized the need for review of abortion as a divisive issue. His interest was shared by James Lipscomb

vii

of the George Gund Foundation. Both the Ford Foundation and the George Gund Foundation made grants in support of this work, but neither of the foundations nor Harkavy or Lipscomb is responsible for its conduct or findings.

The views expressed in this volume are solely those of the authors, and should not be attributed to the trustees, officers, or staff of the Brookings Institution.

BRUCE K. MACLAURY
President

November 1982
Washington, D.C.

Contents

Gilbert Y. Steiner

Introduction: Abortion Policy and the Potential for Mischief

THE DECISIONS of the Supreme Court in 1973 in *Roe* v. *Wade* and *Doe* v. *Bolton* created a national policy on abortion by wiping out preexistent state laws that were distinguishable principally by degree of restrictiveness. Decriminalizing abortion, however, did not wipe out differing judgments about its morality. The firm conviction of most opponents of abortion is that it involves the ultimate immorality—the taking of human life. Because opponents do see abortion in this light, and not just as a simple medical procedure, they expect the coercive authority of government to forbid it. Supporters of legalized abortion deny the premise about the taking of life, and so implicitly dismiss the immorality indictment. For them, abortion is a private medical procedure that a woman may choose to undergo or to reject. In this view, abortion does not belong on the governmental agenda any more than do other surgical procedures that some deem especially unwise. Those discrepant judgments have provoked a politics of abortion that is often viewed as dangerously divisive.

A Troubling Question

Justice William H. Rehnquist in dissent acknowledged that the majority opinion in *Roe* brought "to the decision of this troubling question both extensive historical fact and a wealth of legal scholarship." Right or wrong, the majority opinion is also unambiguous. Seven justices of various political orientations concurred in recognizing and deciding among three distinct rights: the rights of the pregnant woman, the right of the state to promote its interest in maternal health, and the right of the state to promote its interest in the potentiality of human life. The rights of the pregnant woman were given supremacy with the finding of an absolute constitutional protection against state regulation of first trimester abortions. The

1

other rights were acknowledged only with a qualified authorization for states to regulate second trimester abortions and a largely symbolic authorization for unlimited regulation or even proscription of most third trimester abortions. Their legality protected by *Roe*, about 1.5 million abortions are now performed annually.

The specificity of the opinion, its historical and scholarly underpinning, and the strong majority vote in its favor produced neither magnanimity on the winning side nor resignation on the losing side. In Joseph Kraft's words, "abortion is perhaps the most disputed social question in the land today." Despite *Roe*, in one or another form the abortion dispute has continued to confront Congress and congressional candidates, state legislatures, the Court itself, and sundry presidential appointees. Four years and a lot of acrimonious congressional debate after *Roe*, its opponents succeeded in passing the Hyde amendment, a prohibition on the use of federal medical assistance (medicaid) to finance abortions. Three years after that, in a 5–4 decision, the Supreme Court sustained Hyde, thereby giving new strength to the original losers and generating new worry among the original winners. Further conflict, debate, votes, and rulings now appear inevitable on abortion-related questions, including a constitutional prohibition, an easing of restrictions on medicaid financing, and various requirements for second-party notification or consent.

The segment of the population that believes abortion to be immoral believes the Supreme Court to be misguided in providing it constitutional protection. That segment accepts various prohibitions on federal spending for abortion as short-run success and looks to a total prohibition as the ultimate success. The segment of the population that supports the private character of abortion and the Supreme Court decision deplores fiscal and procedural limitations as discriminatory and unwise and looks to universal, unrestricted freedom of choice as its ultimate goal. Since the positions of the respective sides reflect beliefs about two of the most fundamental human values—on the one hand, life, and on the other hand, personal privacy —it should not be surprising that adherents to each position are unyielding. "Abortion can be counted on to be the dominant family-related public problem for the indefinite future," I wrote in *The Futility of Family Policy*, "and the one the policy process is least likely to resolve, because neither side is comfortable with less than total victory, each side views its cause as sacred, and both are right."

Abortion policy has not always enjoyed such prominence. Indeed, for most of the century during which it was both illegal in all of the states and yet widely performed, abortion was far from an everyday subject of public policy debate. A great wave of restrictive state laws enacted in the decade after the Civil War continued in effect for a hundred years, but abortion remained readily available to women who could pay the financial and emotional costs of dealing with the underground. By approximately 1880, James C. Mohr has written, antiabortion forces ceased "to move ever more forcefully against the practice, which they might have done by abrogating the confidentiality of the patient-doctor relationship, or by enforcing the laws against women who sought abortions, or by changing the rules of evidence in abortion trials, or by numerous other means."[1] Whether a sustained effort to destroy the abortion underground could have succeeded is an imponderable. No such effort was made.

Ultimately, some of the justifications given state legislatures for antiabortion law—for example, safety and the need for population growth—became slippery. "Medical imposters" who had done most of the abortion business were driven out by medical professionalizers. Self-abortion, abortion by nonmedical personnel, and abortion by medical personnel acting illegally were the options. Reports persisted of attempts at self-abortion with its attendant dangers. The wide scope of the illegal abortion trade invited a complaint that the law discriminated in favor of those who could afford the high price of an illegal but "safe" abortion. Since most physicians acknowledged that abortion was safe when performed by trained persons, safety was transformed into an argument for legalization. Any lingering concerns about abortion's effects on population growth lost their appeal in the face of startling increases in the birthrate following World War II. Preliminary inroads on state antiabortion laws accomplished during the 1960s culminated in the *Roe* decision that made most abortions legal everywhere in the nation. Abortion policy has since been a constant, explosive issue.

To Improve the Debate and Protect the System

No one dismisses abortion as a trivial question or as one unworthy of careful attention. As advocates on both sides strive to make abortion policy a pervasive question in American politics, many others worry about its divisive impact. This is not to suggest that the losers should quietly fold their tents or that the winners should voluntarily give ground. It is entirely

1. James C. Mohr, *Abortion in America* (Oxford University Press, 1978), p. 245.

appropriate for today's losers to carry on in hopes that they may be tomorrow's winners, just as it is appropriate for today's winners to try to safeguard their success. But it is also important that the battle be fought according to ground rules that protect the American system from long-lasting damage.

What are the potential consequences of the apparently irreconcilable conflict over abortion policy? Prolonged controversy that includes marches, occasional sit-ins, tests of reliability on the issue in the selection and election of public officials, injection of abortion policy into seemingly unrelated aspects of legislative business, and proposals for indirect as well as direct constitutional change all are regarded by some as threats to the American system, shrugged off by others as healthy manifestations of democratic government.

The former view is implicit in a remark made by Senator Barry Goldwater to a *Los Angeles Times* reporter early in 1982 apropos of a colleague's plan to attach abortion restrictions to appropriations bills. "We're more concerned about perpetuation of our form of government than we are with busing, abortion, prayer, or anything else," Goldwater is quoted.[2] Most politicians and most ordinary citizens would probably agree with Goldwater's judgment, yet many would also insist that a concern about abortion need not be incompatible with a concern "about perpetuation of our form of government." Rather, the underlying problem is whether some kinds of strategies used by protagonists of one or another social issue do distort governmental or political institutions and violate the spirit of the American system. The result is two debates—one over the merits of the cause and one over means and whether or not they violate unwritten rules.

The papers in this volume bear on the debate over means and unwritten rules. Abortion policy is the specific point of departure, but the purpose is not to argue the case for or against abortion. Rather, the purpose is to consider whether the relentless pursuit of a policy objective—sometimes using novel or unprecedented techniques—jeopardizes the ability of the governmental system to function. Such political techniques warrant neither condemnation nor admiration simply because they are novel or unprecedented. They do warrant scrutiny because they carry with them a potential for mischief that is nobody's goal.

2. Ellen Hume, *Los Angeles Times*, March 9, 1982. See also Goldwater's statement of September 15, 1981, *Congressional Record*, pp. S9681–82.

McCormick's Rules

Because he found himself disenchanted with "the quality of discourse" about abortion, Richard McCormick, a distinguished Catholic moral theologian, once proposed a set of "rules" for conversation and debate on the subject. Not everything goes, said Father McCormick in effect in a 1978 article that provided some of the intellectual stimulation leading to the work recorded in this volume. As a self-described bone-weary veteran of the abortion dispute, his opinion was that "the sound level rises as verbal bludgeoning and interruptions multiply; the dialogue of the deaf continues."[3] A "chaotic and sclerotic" level of discourse bids fair to destroy "communicative conversation." Neither running from the policy problem nor compromising or abandoning a moral position was held to be a permissible option. But low-quality debate rather than disciplined argument only adds to the costs of the dispute without benefiting either side. Father McCormick's thesis is that no progress is made by substituting slogans for arguments, that the tendency to carry on the abortion debate in a manner that pollutes public discourse is itself deplorable. He suggests consideration of some rules that might benefit all participants. Among his proposed rules for debate are: attempt to identify areas of agreement; represent the opposing position accurately and fairly; avoid the use of slogans; admit doubts, difficulties, and weaknesses in one's own position; distinguish morality and public policy. Attention to these and other such guidelines, Father McCormick wrote, cannot hurt the national debate, and "may prevent good people from making bad arguments."

A reasonable corollary of the thesis and an application of it beyond debate to political activity is that any tendency to engage in the abortion dispute in a manner that distorts the functioning of government institutions is similarly deplorable, perhaps intolerable. Attention to the integrity of governmental institutions cannot hurt the abortion dispute and may prevent good people from taking bad political actions. "There are some prices," as Senator Daniel Patrick Moynihan has said in connection with tactics used in another policy dispute, "too great for no matter what order of victory."

Whether it is time to propose the political action equivalent of Father McCormick's rules for debate depends on whether political behavior in connection with abortion policymaking is—as Father McCormick said of

3. "Abortion: Rules for Debate," *America*, July 22, 1978, reprinted in *Congressional Record* (August 3, 1978), pp. E4312–14.

discourse on the subject—"chaotic and sclerotic." Before proposing his rules, Father McCormick made a persuasive case that disciplined argument on abortion had vanished. Senator Barry Goldwater, in a remark quoted earlier, perceived violations, or planned violations, by pro-life forces of his rules for political activity. His indictment has been made on other occasions as well, but it seems to be based at least as much on stated plans and anticipated behavior as on actual practice. Moreover, the senator's targets deny culpability. There may be grounds for unease about the way the politics of abortion has been pursued. But are there grounds that would justify a finding that the political system is being jeopardized, and that defenders of it should organize a response? It is not a finding to be made casually.

Voluntary Restraint

My assumption is that neither side would knowingly distort a fundamental element of the American governmental system in order to achieve its own objective. There is evidence that over the years of the abortion dispute public persons on each side of the controversy have shied away from strategy that might benefit that side but might also foul the institutions of government. The willingness of many pro-choice congressmen to accept the president's appointment of Surgeon General C. Everett Koop, a pro-life stalwart who was vulnerable on a different, technical count, is a case that Calvin Mackenzie discusses later in this volume. Another example is provided by Senator Mark Hatfield, a devout antiabortionist. Hatfield was an early supporter of a constitutional amendment to prohibit abortion. He is author of a bill to facilitate Supreme Court review of the *Roe* decision and to impose a statutory prohibition on all federal financing of abortions. Nevertheless, as chairman of the Senate Appropriations Committee, he deplores abortion limitations attached to appropriations bills. Hatfield may or may not be unique among congressional antiabortion leaders in a belief that the appropriations rider tactic distorts the proper functioning of the congressional appropriations process. But in speaking out to that effect, Hatfield invites pro-life colleagues in Congress to abandon the most effective weapon in their armamentarium.

An example of concern about a different institution is provided by Senator Orrin Hatch, another confirmed antiabortion policymaker, who described himself as "not yet entirely comfortable" with a bill to provide that human life is deemed to exist from conception. Explaining that his discomfort stems from doubts about constitutionality, Hatch says, "Although I disbelieve in indiscriminate abortion in this country, I believe that the Constitution is the most important political document in the world."[4] For Hatch, it is impermissible to pursue a prohibition on abortion at the expense of what he has termed "sound constitutional principles." It need hardly be added that there are differences of opinion over what are "sound constitutional principles."

Still another example is provided by the behavior of former Secretary of Health, Education, and Welfare Joseph Califano, who was responsible for regulations issued in 1978 to implement some ambiguous language in the Hyde amendment. Califano had stated at his confirmation hearing without qualification that "Federal funds are not appropriate for it, to use Federal funds for an abortion, for women rich or poor." But a year later, Califano said, "My personal views are of no relevance to the legal duty of interpreting what Congress intended and writing regulations that embody that intent."[5] In the event, Califano put his interpretation of congressional intent ahead of his views on abortion. The regulations he approved tilted—within the narrow limits allowed—toward maximizing the abortion possibility.

One more example is provided by Representative Robert Michel, now Republican leader of the House of Representatives. Five years after *Roe* v. *Wade* established national abortion policy, Michel shied away from a constitutional amendment to overturn *Roe* because it conflicts with his view of what belongs in the Constitution: "I personally happen to be one of those individuals who does not like to see our Constitution cluttered up with amendments for busing, for abortion, for booze, or anything else of that nature."[6] Califano, as secretary of HEW, took a similar position: "It does not make any sense that we run to the Constitution on abortion. . . . We have to stop running to the Constitution to solve all of our problems."[7]

A final example is seen in Senator Jake Garn's resignation from the advisory board of the National Pro-Life Political Action Committee in

---

4. *The Human Life Bill*, Hearings before the Subcommittee on Separation of Powers of the Senate Committee on the Judiciary, 97 Cong. 1 sess. (Government Printing Office, 1982), p. 4.

5. *Nominations of Joseph A. Califano, Jr., and Laurence N. Woodworth*, Hearings before the Senate Committee on Finance, 95 Cong. 1 sess. (GPO, 1977), p. 5; and *New York Times*, January 27, 1978.

6. *Departments of Labor and Health, Education, and Welfare Appropriations for 1979*, Hearings before a Subcommittee of the House Committee on Appropriations, 95 Cong. 2 sess. (GPO, 1978), pt. 2, pp. 77–78.

7. *Nominations of Joseph A. Califano, Jr., and Laurence N. Woodworth*, p. 25.

June 1981, after its press conference at which the group announced that it would target several members of the House and Senate for defeat because of their pro-choice position. Garn's own pro-life stand is well known and firm, but he announced himself unalterably opposed to efforts to judge candidates on the basis of a single issue. The practice of single-issue politics, said Garn, "is dangerous to the nation's political health because it too often fosters 'negative tactics.' "[8]

The point to be drawn from the cases cited is that some political leaders do take positions inimical to the interests of the side they favor. They appear to do so out of regard for the integrity of the governmental system. If this integrity is on the whole respected, then there is no cause for concern. But, if most partisans pursue their advocacy without regard for institutions or the prevailing rules of the political game, both sides should be made to think about actual and potential mischiefs of factionalism related to the abortion policy dispute and—if they exist—about how to control their effects.

The Brookings Symposium

Against the background of an intractable dispute, committed antagonists, and public officials concerned about "constitutional clutter" and "single-issue politics," the Brookings Institution invited advocates on both sides of the abortion controversy to join a group of governmental affairs experts—scholars, journalists, congressional staff—in a consideration of the effects of the abortion controversy on the governmental system. The plan for the symposium and the invitation to attend stipulated that it would not address the substantive merits or demerits of abortion. Nor was it the intent of the sponsors to instruct anyone on how to behave. The questions for attention bypassed abortion ideology. Rather, the questions were: Does the dispute have mischievous consequences for the system? If so, what are they? Are they cause for alarm? If so, are there ways to control them without discouraging free debate?

Stated differently, the abortion dispute represents a conflict of ideologies. Ideological conflict may or may not have destructive consequences for governmental institutions. If this conflict does have destructive consequences, those who are not ideologues on this question will take pains to protect any institutions in special jeopardy. If the abortion conflict cannot

8. *National Journal*, October 10, 1981, p. 1814.

be shown to have destructive consequences, neither side need worry about the propriety of its strategy or tactics.

To provide a starting point, Brookings commissioned several scholars who had no history of participation in the abortion controversy to prepare short essays on its apparent consequences for particular aspects of the American system. Each author was able to view the controversy from a fresh vantage point, uncommitted to either a pro-choice or pro-life position. The authors' disciplines include law, political science, and history. Four essays deal with the dispute in a constitutional context and with its effects on the legislative process in Congress, presidential appointments, and popular elections. In addition, because a ban on abortion and Prohibition are sometimes linked as examples of subjects said to be impossible to enforce or somehow unsuitable for a constitution, and whose destructive effects on institutions are said to be as likely after constitutional change as before, an appendix to the volume recalls aspects of the Prohibition experience.

—Lawrence Friedman's examination of the abortion dispute in constitutional context reviews the argument over the "legitimacy" of *Roe* v. *Wade.* He describes the decision as one "of a very select club of Supreme Court decisions that sent shock waves through the country." Friedman asks whether that reaction is attributable to the manner or style in which the decision was written, the way the case was decided, some objection to the Court's having made the decision rather than to the decision itself, or the actual result. Friedman finds no reason to deny the constitutional legitimacy of the decision. Its reasoning, its technique, and its results are not out of line, he says, for our epoch. It is also true, however, that a constitutional amendment overturning the decision would not be an unwarranted "cluttering" of the Constitution. Because the Court put abortion into the Constitution, the Constitution is the only available battleground. No theory good enough to win widespread approval defines what is a "proper" subject for the written Constitution or what is a "legitimate" Supreme Court decision.

Friedman contends that the Court knew what it was doing in *Roe.* It rested the decision on a base of prior law and produced a decision that in form was highly legalistic. The Court is not locked in, however, and no one can say how it would respond to a congressional attempt to undo what *Roe* has done. Friedman's paper begins by comparing the debate over *Roe* to that over *Brown* v. *Board of Education* or *Dred Scott*, two cases reflecting disputes that did have important consequences for the American system. But by the end of the paper, readers will infer that *Roe* put neither the Constitution nor the Court in jeopardy.

—Roger Davidson suggests abortion to be an issue that has consumed a good deal of congressional time and has given Congress great trouble because there is no "comfortable" middle ground. As a consequence, it is difficult if not impossible to make the accommodations that are a necessary part of the effective functioning of Congress. From Davidson's account, I conclude that neither the prohibitionists nor their opponents have been models of fairness in manipulating congressional consideration of a public policy problem of acknowledged importance to many Americans. Conservatives, recently come to power in the Senate, failed to accord deference to the judgment of the Supreme Court about the meaning of the Constitution. By proposing to overturn that judgment with ordinary legislation of doubtful merit, they stretched the rules. By seeming to rush along that path without listening to contrary views, they further stretched the rules. By proposing constitutional change without getting agreement among themselves on a course of action, they may have again stretched the rules, given the usual disposition to regard constitutional change as reflecting a broad consensus of opinion.

On the other side, liberal opponents of a prohibition on abortion also seem to have been guilty of ignoring some unwritten rules—most particularly in failing to have given the opposition a hearing to which it was probably entitled in the late 1970s if public interest, importance of subject, and volume of proposed legislation are fair tests.

But these are not matters of major moment that constitute perversion of parliamentary law. Moreover, in explaining the extensive use pro-life legislators have made of appropriations limitations in order to deny or restrict federal financing of abortions, Davidson shows the technique to be in the mainstream of recent congressional processes and not a unique threat to orderly procedures.

Passionate conviction is the enemy of orderly legislative procedure, Davidson warns. When one prevails, the other suffers. While Davidson believes that "legislative processes have not done justice to the gravity and complexity of abortion as a public policy problem," he does not find that passionate conviction about abortion has actually jeopardized orderly procedure.

—Calvin Mackenzie discusses the handful of recent cases in which a presidential appointee's views on abortion have been an important issue. No potential appointee has failed to be confirmed because of a stance on abortion. At the extreme, only two dozen votes were cast against a nominee, C. Everett Koop, and it is virtually impossible to separate the votes cast against him because of his abortion views from those cast against him because of his age or his lack of experience in public health. Significantly, the other celebrated case involving a nominee's abortion views ended with a unanimous vote of the Senate in favor of Justice Sandra O'Connor's confirmation—suggesting that the issue can be transcended.

Abortion politics, however, runs against the grain of the traditional politics of the appointment process, according to Mackenzie. Coalition building and negotiated settlement of diverse perspectives are the forerunners of agreement on appointments, but the mutually exclusive views on abortion make this traditional process difficult. Good luck and special circumstances have kept the abortion dispute from bringing delay, stalemate, and acrimony to the appointment process.

Maybe luck will hold and all circumstances will be special, but Mackenzie would prefer acceptance of two ground rules, "not only for continued effectiveness of the appointment process, but also for it to contribute to the reasonable conduct of the national debate over abortion policy."

His first rule provides that an appointee's personal views on abortion should be allowed to become a significant factor in selection and confirmation only where the position involved has some jurisdiction over abortion policy. The second rule holds that even where the position does have jurisdiction over abortion policy, more should be considered than just the appointee's views on abortion. Taken together, Mackenzie's findings and rules present a plea for caution and realism—caution lest imprecise recollections of hard cases result in unwarranted judgments about distortion of the system, realism lest the scant evidence to date lead to a belief that there is no need to plan for the future.

—John Jackson and Maris Vinovskis review what is known about abortion as a "single issue" affecting public opinion and elections. They are concerned especially with the putative growth of single-issue electoral politics in which abortion is said to be the factor controlling voting decisions. The authors show first the complex task involved in determining what public opinion is about abortion. In addition to the variations in responses attributable to the wording of questions or the order in which questions are posed, analysis of opinion must deal with such nuances as relative intensity of feeling and consistency of attitude under various conditions.

While numbers of voters holding a particular opinion are important, where the voters are may be equally important in evaluating the impact of the issue on electoral results. If a small minority with firm views were concentrated in certain areas, it could exercise more influence on elections in those areas than on elections in the country as a whole. Jackson and Vinovskis find, in fact, that there are only small differences in the geographic characteristics of pro-life and pro-choice populations.

The widely discussed single-issue phenomenon that attributes electoral outcomes to a candidate's abortion stance is challenged by the authors' empirical review of post-*Roe* congressional elections. They believe the tendency to link the pro-life cause with political conservatism and the pro-choice cause with political liberalism will tie the fortunes of these causes to those of the broader political movements. As one or the other movement prospers or falters so may the cause tied to it.

All in all, Jackson and Vinovskis see little threat to the political system from abortion as a single issue. The American system of single-winner, plurality-determined elections requires the eventual formation of coalitions with bases broader than any single issue. Abortion has been and is one among many separate issues that collectively determine electoral results.

—Cynthia Harrison's historical note on the Prohibition experience serves as a reminder of troubles associated with a previous effort to regulate conduct by constitutional restraint. This is not to say that comparable troubles must follow any constitutional prohibition of previously allowable behavior. There are not grounds for such a judgment. But Harrison's note helps sharpen attention to strains on the system that could develop following a major policy change.

The analyses and conclusions summarized above point to an apparent unanimity of judgment among the contributors. They find the abortion dispute divisive, but not a real and present danger to governmental institutions. Actions of the groups seeking to influence the decision—or change the decision—about abortion policy have not jeopardized the American system. Policy decisions have been reached pursuant to traditional political procedures.

This sanguine view reflects the editor's interpretation of the essays that follow. The views of the diverse group of activists attending the Brookings symposium are summarized later in the volume under the title "Reactions of the Symposium."

Lawrence M. Friedman

The Conflict over Constitutional Legitimacy

THE *Roe* v. *Wade* decision was controversial in 1973, and it is just as controversial today—if not more so. Few cases have led to as much hot and bitter debate. For parallels, one may have to reach back to *Brown* v. *Board of Education*, or perhaps all the way to *Dred Scott. Roe* v. *Wade* belongs to a very select club of Supreme Court decisions—those that sent shock waves through the country, affecting every aspect of political life. How one assesses this impact, and its political consequences, depends in part on how one looks at *Roe* v. *Wade*. Does it lie outside the mainstream of constitutional doctrine? Or is it not out of line—for the present epoch at least—in doctrine or theory?

The Question of Legitimacy

What was it about *Roe* v. *Wade* that touched off such a storm of comment and criticism? Some critics claim to be bothered not by the outcome, but by what they consider poor craftsmanship. For others the objection is more fundamental. They challenge the very legitimacy of *Roe*. They find no warrant in the Constitution for what the Court did; abortion, they think, has no business parading before society as a constitutional issue. Louis Lusky has described *Roe* v. *Wade*, sneeringly, as "freehand constitution-making."[1] Other scholars have said even worse things about it. Senator Jesse Helms summarized the views of seven eminent constitutional scholars, who all expressed "shock and dismay" over the reasoning of the Court. Helms was able to fill his statement with quotes that condemned the case: it was a mere "political judgment," or even "the most outrageous decision ever handed down by the Court."

Of course, many scholars defend the decision. Some of these take a

---

1. *By What Right?* (Michie/Bobbs-Merrill, 1975), p. 14.

13

position which is almost the polar opposite. They are dismayed by attempts to undo *Roe* v. *Wade* by amending the Constitution. They, too, talk about legitimacy, but for them it is such an amendment that would be illegitimate. Abortion, they say, does not belong in our written Constitution, which should stick to more fundamental matters.

I find it hard to accept either view—that the Court was wrong to interpret the Constitution as it did, or contrariwise, that it would be wrong to amend the Constitution to go back to the days before *Roe*. The first view is historically naive. It is based on a theory of what the Court is and does that bursts like a soap bubble when one looks at the record over time. The second viewpoint is strategically appealing, but is, alas, rather illogical. After all, it was *Roe* v. *Wade* that put abortion rights into the Constitution. If it was legitimate for the Court to do this, it can hardly be illegitimate to take *Roe* out through the amendment process.

Numerous critics are convinced that the Court transgressed against something; yet the error is rather elusive. There is no real agreement about what was transgressed. One claim, put bluntly, is that it went beyond the legitimate role of the Supreme Court. But it is hard to say what that role is. Nearly everybody agrees that the Court should decide its cases according to law, or reason, or policy, or principle, and not indulge the mere personal preferences of the judges. Every serious scholar of the Court would also agree that the Court does not and cannot simply "interpret" what the Constitution says. The Court goes far beyond the words of the text and has been doing so since at least the days of John Marshall. Dozens of scholars have tried to work out some theory or other to justify the Court's behavior and (more significantly) to find some line that separates "correct" or "legitimate" decisions from the other kind. I think it is fair to say that nobody has succeeded. At the very least, it seems clear that nobody has come up with a theory good enough to win general approval.

The point is important. There is a general question about the constitutional work of the Court and how it can be justified, a question that goes far beyond the abortion case and attaches itself to most of what the Court has done for decades. Some critics of the Court throw around the word *countermajoritarian*. Nobody elects the Supreme Court, and nobody can unelect a justice once he or she takes a seat on the bench. The idea is then that the Court's enormous power is discordant or suspicious in a democratic country.

I do not dismiss this argument out of hand. But the "democracy" that critics talk about is much too simple a picture of the modern state. It has little to do with our very different and very complicated system of government that works in all sorts of strange, unpredicted, and unpredictable ways. Certainly, the Court often blocks action that some other branch of government wants to take. Is this undemocratic? It may be, but is it less democratic than the acts of some low-level bureaucrat whose claim to democracy is that he was appointed by someone, who was in turn appointed by somebody else, who was himself appointed by somebody actually elected at the polls?

Our system gives a great deal of power to judges, with little formal control over them, and there may be a lot wrong with that. But that system has evolved over the years, for better or for worse, along with the administrative system itself. After all, modern government is also big and powerful; all branches may abuse their power. The courts in this society are locked in a complicated relationship with government at all levels. The general legitimacy of the Supreme Court's decisions may be fair game for attack in any total review of the American system. Problems of general legitimacy, however, are not grounds for objecting to a single decision—not even this one.

Roe v. *Wade* and Its Forebears

The more immediate, special question is whether the abortion case stands out from other major decisions. Is it illegitimate in a special or more egregious way than the rest? It has been argued that the case is indeed out of line—in its reasoning, its technique, its results. I look to see if this is so.

At issue in *Roe* v. *Wade* was a Texas law that made abortion a crime except "for the purpose of saving the life of the mother." Justice Harry A. Blackmun, in his majority opinion, detailed the history of abortion law in the United States, partly to show that abortion had not always been a crime. He then referred to a "right to privacy" (or "zones of privacy") protected by the Constitution. The right, he said, was "broad enough to encompass a woman's decision whether or not to terminate her pregnancy."

That right, however, was not "absolute." For one thing, the pregnant woman is not "isolated in her privacy." Life stirs inside her. The state has an interest in protecting that life, and it also has an interest in protecting the mother's health. All these considerations have to be balanced somehow. The Court's solution was to split pregnancy into three trimesters. In the first of these, the woman's right to choose an abortion was fairly absolute.

In the second trimester, the state could regulate, "reasonably," in the interests of "maternal health." In the last three months, when the unborn baby
becomes "viable," the state may step in to protect its interests, even going
so far as to forbid abortion completely.

Obviously, the Texas law did not measure up to these standards. No
statute could, at the time. (A companion case, *Doe* v. *Bolton*, struck down a
Georgia statute far more liberal than the one in Texas.) Thus in one bold,
cataclysmic move the Court undid about a century of legislative action. It
swept away every abortion law in the country, just as in the first death
penalty case the Court undid all capital punishment laws and emptied
every death house in the land. No wonder these cases made headlines.

Interestingly, the Court was not closely divided in *Roe* v. *Wade*. Seven
justices joined on the majority side; only two justices dissented. The majority clearly thought it had reached a fair compromise. For example, some of
the groups leading the attack on abortion laws wanted an absolute right to
abort, from conception to the bitter end. The Court turned down this idea
in favor of its timetable plan. The chief justice, concurring in *Bolton*, made
clear that the Court "rejected" any idea that "the Constitution requires
abortion on demand." Bold the case was, and surprising, perhaps. But not,
the Court felt, out of line, not unreasonable.

A common-law legal system means, among other things, that doctrine
creeps forward incrementally, case building on case. Constitutional adjudi-
cation is supposed to be different, but in reality it is not. In fact, *Roe* v.
Wade did rest, if a mite precariously, on a basis of prior cases. The most
important was *Griswold* v. *Connecticut*, the famous birth control decision.
Griswold struck down a Connecticut law that said, among other things,
that "Any person who uses any drug . . . or instrument for the purpose of
preventing conception" could be fined or put in jail. Justice William O.
Douglas's opinion talked about a constitutional right of privacy, or a "zone
of privacy" protected by the Constitution. At the end of his opinion, he
waxed eloquent on the subject of married love, and its "sacred . . . har-
mony." He was protecting, he felt, a right of privacy far "older than the Bill
of Rights."

Griswold talked privacy, but it was not clear exactly what was private
and why. The Connecticut law restricted, among other things, the "use" of
contraceptives. Any serious attempt to enforce this kind of law really would
breach people's privacy, and in the grossest possible way. After all, most
married people committed the "crime" in the dark of night, and in the
"sacred" precincts of their bedrooms.

But was this really the message of *Griswold*? Not as the Court itself understood it. The Court was groping toward an important new idea, but it was unclear where or how far it would run with it. In *Eisenstadt v. Baird*, the Court considered a Massachusetts law that, among other things, allowed only doctors or druggists to distribute contraceptives and only to married people. Baird, the defendant, gave a lecture on the subject of contraception and when he was done handed out a sample to a woman in the audience. He was arrested and convicted, but the Supreme Court overturned his conviction. The statute was unconstitutional.

Eisenstadt clearly went beyond *Griswold*. The earlier case had put heavy stress on the marital relationship, but the Court saw no reason to draw a decisive line between married and unmarried people. If *Griswold* meant that the state could not ban distribution of contraceptives to married people, it must imply that distribution could not be banned at all. The right of privacy was an individual right, shared by husband and wife, and if so, there was no reason to limit the right to married people. (Notice the shift from "use" to "distribution" of contraceptives.) Again, one has to ask: what is this right of privacy? The *Eisenstadt* case, after all, had nothing to do with snooping around bedrooms.

In both cases, of course, the justices wrote many separate opinions, and they did tend to go on at great length. They said so many things that the cases are a little like Rorschach's inkblots. But this in itself is important, just as it was important that seven out of nine judges agreed—even if they could not agree on why they agreed—in both *Griswold* and in *Roe v. Wade*. They knew at least what result they wanted, though not the right way to get there.

These cases, then, are not about a constitutional right of privacy at all, even though they talk this language. They are about something else, much vaguer, which one commentator has called "sexual liberty" and another protection of "personal matters" that do not involve, and hence go "beyond," the "public welfare."

Clearly these cases do concern sex, marriage, and reproduction. On the evidence of the *Griswold* line of cases, an outside observer could guess correctly that sexual morality and sexual life-styles are big issues in the United States today. In the years since *Griswold*, the Supreme Court and other high federal courts have decided many cases on sex, sexuality, marriage, family living, and personal life-styles—ranging all over the lot and dealing not only with birth control and abortion, but also with the right to marry, zoning restrictions on different kinds of "family," gay rights, forni-

cation, and so on. Where the decisions end up is not easy to say. On the
surface, an argument can be made that the Court has pitched its tent in the
camp of the most "advanced" elements of American society. But there is
evidence on the other side as well. For example, the Court has refused to
strike down sodomy statutes. Thomas C. Grey, for one, detects in the
Court's work a pattern of deep respect for the traditional family, and for
traditional family values, though in modern dress.[2] I will return to this
point.

The Social Issue

The Supreme Court picks its cases; but it picks them from among the
hundreds that come up from below, clamoring for attention. These cases, in
the aggregate, represent what troubles society. In a sense, then, the court's
agenda is always fresh. It is always a kind of menu of issues, faithful more
or less to what is brewing in society.

Griswold and *Roe* are about social issues; indeed, the abortion decision
is perhaps the key social issue today. But exactly what is the issue? A good
way to begin is to define what it is not. It is not permissiveness as such, or
the vexed question of sexual morality. At any rate, that is not what the
Supreme Court is up to. There is no evidence that the Court wants to read
the "sexual revolution" into the Constitution, or to discover the philosophy
of *Playboy* magazine hidden in the text of the Fourteenth Amendment.
The Court is not even embracing the old-fashioned liberalism of John Stu-
art Mill. Nor is it accepting, as dogma or working principle, the idea that
whatever consenting adults do to or with each other in private and without
violence is beyond the reach of the state.

Indeed, Thomas Grey, in his insightful essay, argues that the Court is
playing a rather conservative game. It is trying to preserve family values in
a confused and complicated world. The contraception and abortion cases,
he says, are "dedicated to the cause of social stability through the rein-
forcement of traditional institutions." They have "nothing to do with the
sexual liberation of the individual. The contraception and abortion cases
are simply family planning cases." In particular, they represent a "stan-

2. "Eros, Civilization and the Burger Court," *Law and Contemporary Problems*, vol. 43
(Summer 1980), p. 83.

dard conservative" view, that "family stability is threatened by unwanted pregnancies."[3]

On issues of sex, marriage, abortion, and the rest, there are, of course, all sorts of views in society; and we can label these views (with some rough accuracy) as right, left, and various degrees of middle. The Supreme Court —judging from the results of its decisions—lies somewhere in the middle of the range of opinion. It is of course light-years away from the fundamentalists in the Bible Belt, yet Grey's point is still a good one. The Supreme Court has shown sympathy and respect for traditional family values. It recognizes, however, that today's traditional family is different from yesterday's and has to be different to survive.

What the justices think about social issues may be less important than what they think about the role of their court. Here we have to read the record carefully and between the lines. (Often one does best by refusing to read the opinions at all, on the grounds that outcomes tell more about what the justices are up to than do endless pages of constitutional "filler.") The justices seem to feel that cases like *Griswold* and *Wade* have a special quality that sets them apart from other public issues. In some significant way, society should not or cannot trust the usual decisionmakers (legislators, for example) in these affairs. This point is worth exploring.

In *Cleveland Board of Education* v. *LaFleur*, teachers in two school districts asked the Court to overturn certain school board rules about teachers who became pregnant. In Cleveland these teachers had to give notice of their condition and go on leave without pay after four or five months of pregnancy. There were also restrictive rules about how long teachers had to wait after giving birth before they could return to the job. The excuses given—concern for the teachers' health, continuity in teaching —seem flimsy at best. The Court struck down these rules, finding no justification for them. (The exact grounds are not important here.) And, at the level of the Supreme Court, there was barely any mention of what probably were the real reasons for the rules.

These real reasons rested on two kinds of prudery, one general, one specific to schools. Potter Stewart's majority opinion refers to them in a single footnote. The original inspiration for the regulations, Stewart writes, was different from the reasons the School Board subsequently advanced, or at least the record so suggested. Stewart quoted the words of a former school superintendent in Cleveland, who testified about saving pregnant

3. Ibid., pp. 83, 88.

teachers "from embarrassment at the hands of giggling schoolchildren." The rules were meant to get rid of teachers who were beginning "to show." In the companion case, from Chesterfield County, Virginia, members of the School Board testified about "insulating" children "from the sight of conspicuously pregnant women." One member thought it was "not good for the school system" if the "kids" saw pregnant teachers, and he worried that some of them might say "my teacher swallowed a watermelon, things like that."

The school boards did not argue (Stewart adds) that "these considerations can serve as a legitimate basis for a rule requiring pregnant women to leave work; we thus note the comments only to illustrate the possible role of outmoded taboos in the adoption of the rules." The taboos, of course, were not just taboos about pregnancy; they were also taboos about how the schools should approach (or avoid) anything to do with sexuality. In spirit, the rules in *LaFleur* were not unlike rules that once kept married students out of high school or, when these failed in court, tried to keep them off baseball and football teams, away from proms, and out of social activities generally. In one of these cases, *Indiana High School Athletic Association v. Raike*, it was said that married students might damage the "integrity and wholesome atmosphere of amateur high school athletics"; married students would be "bad examples" with an "unwholesome influence." They might, after all, discuss "marital intimacies" and come up with other kinds of "corrupting 'locker room talk.' "

A phrase like "Victorian prudery" does not properly capture the attitude here. The rules in these cases embody a theory of the place of schools in our society: schools should represent the ideals of chastity and morality, obedience and respect for authority. Whether the ideals are outmoded or the rules so inappropriate that they do more harm than good are matters of debate, but there is surely doubt about whether school boards have any business fostering these ideals through rigid rules. Clearly, the Supreme Court felt the school rules were out of place.

One of the historic functions of judicial review is the sort of clean-up function that *LaFleur* represents. The courts—from the lowest to the highest—sit in review of administrative behavior, including the thousands of rules and regulations that pour out of Washington, the fifty state capitals, and the many city halls, not to mention zoning boards, school districts, transport and sewer authorities, occupational licensing commissions, and all the rest. Many of the laws and regulations are unfair; many of them represent "outmoded taboos." The courts are the broom that sweeps them away. The measuring rods are very vague, very broad principles. These are attached loosely to phrases in the Constitution. They are connected more organically to the general culture. This connection is neither formal nor "legal"; it rests on the fact that judges live in society and take their values from society.

But if the taboos in cases like *LaFleur* are so outmoded, why do school boards hold on to them? What keeps such relics alive? Administrative convenience is part of the answer. The bureaucracy benefits from the rules and thus has an interest in retaining them. Beyond that, however, are political and structural impediments. Legislators have no time or patience for reviewing thousands of local rules or bureaucratic abuses. That job historically has been left to the courts.

Roe v. *Wade*, of course, is a different matter. Here the Court upset solemn acts of state legislatures. When the case was decided, there were abortion laws everywhere, and the issue was not unknown, low key, or invisible. Yet only the Court could have gotten rid of the abortion laws. Only the Court—though this is less clear—could have gotten rid of the outmoded law in *Griswold*. Just so, says the majoritarian, who enters a plausible protest. Granted that only the justices could get rid of such "outmoded taboos" without ruining their careers in the process. Isn't this precisely the objection? If a legislator would be thrown out of office for voting to repeal a law like the one in *Griswold*, doesn't this mean that the public favors the law—that it does not want the law repealed? It may, of course, mean exactly that.

But it also may not. It is conceivable that most people in Connecticut—and most legislators—were glad to have the Court do the dirty work. In a pluralist system there are many laws that could not now be passed as an initial matter and yet cannot now be repealed. On some highly controverted subjects, the status quo is frozen; to move up or down, forward or backward, is politically dangerous. Major abortion law falls in that class. The only safe course is doing nothing. In 1973, it was hard to move on abortion in any direction. For the most part this is still true a decade later. Despite the activity of pro-life groups and the support of the president, antiabortion law moves very slowly in Congress. There is more action in the states, but hardly a landslide. New laws show recalcitrance, but not outright defiance. The most sensitive issues are those that touch on the rights of parents. Teenage sex clearly troubles people far more than whether a husband and wife decide on an abortion. Legislators, on the whole (one suspects), would be pleased if the whole issue could somehow go away.

There is a package of social issues about which people are likely to hide their real feelings. Pornography is one. Prostitution is another. Both are big businesses. Few people speak up for them, certainly few congressmen. That there are so many customers, however, means there is a large, hidden interest group, whose impact is felt but not heard. Abortion may not be in the same camp, but there are definite similarities. Few people are *for* abortion. Rather, they accept it as a necessary evil. The arguments against abortion are direct, simple, and to the point. The arguments for it are indirect and complicated. They are less arguments for abortion than against forbidding it, and for reasons other than the merits of abortion. (Similarly, very few people defend pornography. Instead, they defend the right of free speech, and try to sneak pornography into this tent.)

The court's opinion in *Roe* v. *Wade* seems to take these factors into account. It was an attempt to wipe out what the Court considered outmoded taboos, in a field where, for various political and social reasons, legislative action was difficult, if not impossible; to frame a relatively clearcut, objective rule; to compromise between extremists on both sides; and to put the issue to rest. These were old and useful aims, by and large, that had worked many times before. *Griswold*, for example, is a case in point. By 1973, contraception was hardly an issue. The Court had helped put it to rest.

The Response to *Roe* v. *Wade*

What *Roe* did, in essence, was to take a social problem and reduce it to a legal problem, at least in form. The technique does not always work. It failed in *Dred Scott*, for example. But there the Court failed because it came out on the wrong side of the issue, not because of form or technique. The solution was unacceptable to a large, passionate, committed group of people. The Court can do a lot, but it cannot control passions that run deep enough to bring on war. The abortion decision may be of this type, but there is good reason to doubt it.

I have argued that the abortion case did not come out of the blue. It rested on a base of prior law. The prior law was rather porous and spongy, but it was there, at least from *Griswold* on. The Court did not jump into the abortion decision feet first. It went slowly and carefully, did considerable soul-searching, and came out with a decision that in form was highly legalistic. The Court acted, as it always does, in the classic common-law way, building on the base of the past.

The abortion issue, however, turned out to be more difficult than the Court expected. The decision provoked enormous controversy. The reaction was volcanic—a slow rumble, followed by eruptions. No one predicted so strong a response. Yet after a decade, the controversy is still essentially legal and electoral. Nobody has taken to the street. Compared to the aftermath of *Brown* v. *Board of Education*, for example, the reaction to *Roe* v. *Wade*—for all its sound and fury—has been relatively toothless. There has been no special, thorough attack on the Court—not, at any rate, because of this case alone. There are some proposals to tinker with its jurisdiction. But the Court has not been a lightning rod for accumulated furies, as was true of the race cases. The reaction, in short, although loud and continuous, has also been solidly normal and well within the ground rules of debate. There is no reason to doubt it will continue to be so.

The abortion cases after *Roe* show the Court in a cautious mood. This may have helped to defuse the controversy. The Court stuck to its guns at first. In *Planned Parenthood of Missouri* v. *Danforth*, the Court confronted a Missouri law passed a year after *Roe*. Among other things, it required a married woman to get her husband's consent before an abortion. Unmarried women under eighteen had to get parental consent. The Court struck down these rules. Another part of the statute outlawed "saline amniocentesis, as a method or technique of abortion, after the first twelve weeks of pregnancy." This was, in fact, the most common technique in medical use at the time. The Court struck down this restriction too. It was "unreasonable"—a "regulation designed to inhibit . . . the vast majority of abortions after the first twelve weeks." Six justices joined in the decision one way or another. The *Wade* court held firm, except for the chief justice.

Firmness (of a sort) also characterized *Bellotti* v. *Baird*, a case which involved the vexing question of abortion for teenaged girls. A Massachusetts law, enacted against the background of *Danforth*, required the consent of the girls' parents. If "one or both" refused, a judge of the superior court could give consent, "for good cause shown, after such hearing as he deems necessary." The Massachusetts legislature was obviously trying to discourage abortion and to make a statement about parents' rights, the family, and the like. The Court did not go along. The statute was, in effect, labeled a nice try, but it fell "short of constitutional standards in certain respects." Every minor must have the right "to go directly to a court without first consulting or notifying her parents." If she convinces the court that she is "mature" and can make an "intelligent" abortion choice on her own, the court "must" allow her to act, "without parental consultation or consent."

The case had no real majority opinion. The language quoted came from Justice Lewis F. Powell, Jr., joined by the chief justice, Potter Stewart, and (surprisingly) William H. Rehnquist, who had been a dissenter in both *Roe* and *Danforth*, but was willing to go along with the Court as long as *Danforth* lasted. Another group of four justices concurred in the result. Only Justice Byron R. White dissented. The various opinions refer at times to the "constitutional right" to have an abortion, but the Constitution itself is not cited. This is yet another sign of what one might call the common-law approach to constitutional law. The abortion case grew out of the *Griswold* line and then established a new starting point, on which still later cases built, one on top of the other. This method is time-honored, a classic technique of legal evolution. Constitutional theory tends to ignore it, and constitutional decisions are supposed to be special, because they rest on a text, and a sacred one at that. But the actual process of decision is much the same as in other fields of law.

The latest word, and a most ambiguous one, came in 1981 in *H. L.* v. *Matheson*, a case from Utah. This too had to do with the duty to notify parents. The plaintiff wanted the Court to strike down the Utah statute but the Court dodged the issue. The opinion, written by Chief Justice Warren E. Burger, upheld the statute as it applied to the plaintiff, a girl who lived with her parents, was not emancipated, and made "no claim or showing as to her maturity or . . . her relations with her parents." For such people, the statute was constitutional, and the Court did not have to ask whether the law was offensive when applied to young women in other situations. The case looks like a cautious, strategic retreat from the exposed ground occupied in *Bellotti*, but nobody can be sure as yet where the Court is going.

The cases clearly are part of a complex ritual dance between the Court and the state legislatures. Massachusetts, Missouri, Utah, and other states had been squirming and wriggling to find ways around some aspects of *Roe* v. *Wade*. The states used standard methods—methods that are, in the long run, fairly innocuous. Essentially, the legislatures comb through opinions, looking for chinks in the armor. The results, even when the Court accepts them, are a kind of compromise: for example, teenage versus adult abortion. A similar pattern is evident as the states have tried to wriggle and squirm out of the death penalty cases. Again, the results are mixed. The latest death penalty laws are different from the old ones and concede a lot to the doctrines the Court has imposed.

The Court itself is also willing to bend. Even the "firm" cases have had elements of compromise. The *Danforth* case specifically approved of some aspects of the Missouri law; the *Bellotti* case did the same for the Massachusetts statute.

The Funding Cases

The abortion funding cases give off an even stronger odor of compromise. *Danforth* and *Bellotti* disappointed the right to life movement but the cases on public funding have given it more reason for cheer. In *Beal* v. *Doe*, the issue was the power of a state to control abortion money under medicaid (title XIX of the Social Security Act). According to federal law, participating states had to establish "reasonable standards . . . for determining . . . the extent of medical assistance" under state medicaid plans. Pennsylvania issued regulations that limited abortions under the program to those "deemed medically necessary." A 6–3 majority of the Court decided that Pennsylvania's rule was "not inconsistent with Title XIX." Strictly speaking, the case simply interpreted what Congress meant when it talked about "standards."

A companion case, *Maher* v. *Roe*, met the constitutional question head on. The case was brought by (or in the name of) two indigent women in Connecticut, Mary Poe, a sixteen-year-old high school junior, and Susan Roe, an unwed mother of three children. In Connecticut, medicaid paid for childbirth expenses, but not for abortions, even in the first trimester, unless "medically necessary." This distinction (or discrimination) between two classes of poor women was challenged as a violation of the equal protection clause of the Constitution.

This argument was certainly plausible, and the Court could have struck down the Connecticut rules—if it wanted to. It did not. The Court reasoned that Connecticut put no "obstacles" in the way of abortion and did not "impinge" on rights recognized in *Roe* v. *Wade*. The state simply refused to pay, and thus chose to encourage childbirth. That was its privilege. On the same day, the Court, in a short, swift opinion (*Poelker* v. *Doe*), upheld a "directive" from the mayor of St. Louis that prohibited abortion in city hospitals "except when there was a threat of grave physiological injury or death to the mother."

Then in 1980 the Hyde amendment—a prohibition on the expenditure of federal medicaid money for most abortions—was narrowly sustained (5–4) in *Harris* v. *McRae*. The majority cited the earlier funding cases. In those cases, it was the *state* that chose not to pay for abortions. Here the federal government imposed that choice on the states. A majority saw no difference in principle. The veterans of *Maher* dissented again, together with Stevens. They stressed that the Hyde amendment was more extreme than the state regulations upheld in the earlier cases. Hyde required danger to the life of the mother. By implication, dangers to the mother's health, mental or physical, were not enough to justify spending federal money on abortion.

The funding cases are best understood as a kind of compromise. They may not be good compromise or fair compromise (women with money can do as they wish; the poor are out of luck); but they are compromise all the same. The Court is, no doubt, shocked by the passions let loose by *Roe* v. *Wade*. But the justices believe in that decision and see no reason to turn back. As they ride out the storm of public opinion, they look on the funding cases as ballast to be thrown overboard. Whether the storm gods will be satisfied with these actions remains to be seen.

Stability and Change

What is the future of abortion law? There are proposals to strip federal courts of jurisdiction in abortion cases, but these seem doomed to fail. *Roe* v. *Wade* will continue to be the law unless the Supreme Court overrules itself or is overruled by constitutional amendment or otherwise. One mechanism to turn the Court around is a proposed statute that would declare, as the sense of Congress, that human life exists from the moment of conception. Congress is empowered to enforce the Fourteenth Amendment by appropriate legislation; thus Congress could (arguably) prohibit abortion as a way of protecting "life." If the Court went along, this would be the end of *Roe* v. *Wade*.

This seems too tricky a route to those who favor formal constitutional amendment, a more cumbersome but forthright technique. An amendment to the Constitution would at least eliminate one imponderable, namely, whether the Court would uphold a human life bill as constitutional. Supporters of the statutory approach think constitutional amendment is too slow and too likely to fail. And some opponents of abortion, like former

Secretary of Health, Education, and Welfare Joseph A. Califano, feel that constitutional amendment would be somehow inappropriate. "We have to stop running to the Constitution to solve all of our problems," Califano has said.

Is it out of bounds to write abortion into the Constitution? This question cannot be sensibly answered as a matter of theory. What is appropriate for a constitution is whatever is perceived as fundamental and important. The Constitution protects life, liberty, and property. For those who feel strongly that abortion is murder, it is absurd to argue that the subject is not appropriate. Understandably, the pro-choice people oppose an abortion amendment and use all arguments, including those of constitutional purity. As I noted earlier, it was the Court that put the abortion issue into the Constitution. The opponents have no choice but to fight on the battlefield imposed on them. The real issue, the issue that cannot be avoided, is the morality and social utility of abortion itself.

Again, it is not helpful to argue in a technical, legal way about congressional power to enact a human life statute. The issue at stake is not one of nice legalisms. A law that declares the sense of Congress to be that life begins at conception is a law that declares the sense of Congress to be that the abortion decision is wrong and should be overturned. The Supreme Court would get this message and would have to decide on its own response. Such a law would not simply "correct" a wrong reading of the Constitution. It would try to strip the Court of some power as a way of undoing an unpopular decision.

This is not the first time Congress has been disappointed or dismayed by Court decisions. Congress has occasionally responded by passing a law to undo the decision. Sometimes the Court accepts Congress's verdict, and sometimes it does not. I pass over the details, but one example of the latter is the 1922 child labor tax case. This upset an attempted end run around *Hammer* v. *Dagenhart*, the odious 1918 case in which the Court struck down a federal child labor law on interstate commerce grounds.

The attitude of the Court toward laws passed to get around doctrinal hurdles is not predictable. Outcomes depend very little on the technical beauty of the devices. They depend a lot on the strength of the public reaction to the Court's line, and on how strongly the Court is attached to the doctrine or decision that Congress attacks. That in turn depends on who the nine justices are at the time. In short, one can say nothing definite on the subject. This has not prevented all sorts of self-serving predictions.

Most constitutional experts are doctrinalists. Their strength is their grasp of the Court's legal language. But constitutional discourse is more a barrier than a help to discussion. Judges and scholars speak a kind of foreign language. It is a conventional language, and has a certain hypnotic charm. It has little to do with the actual thoughts of actors in the system. Many scholars believe that the power, prestige, and legitimacy of the Court depend on the grammar of this language—that if the Court departs from convention, in word or deed, and begins speaking English, it is inevitably doomed.

There is no hard evidence to support this view. My own notion is the opposite. The power, prestige, and legitimacy of the Court depend mostly on what it does. If the Court sits high, it is because it has staked out a position of bold moral authority. The public thinks better of its motives than those of politicians. And the public is not wholly wrong. The Court may not be "bound" in the naive sense some people think it is. It is bound by its very freedom and power—bound to move carefully, bound to consider the consequences of its acts. In some curious way, the public may understand this. And in some curious way, the Court may command the most respect precisely when it is most dramatically "countermajoritarian." As I have argued, the "majority" here may be, in part, an illusion. A large silent group feels that *Roe* v. *Wade* is wise and just. The Court is its outlet, its spokesman. The Court has been, on the whole, rather moderate and cautious. But the future course of the abortion dispute is likely to be troubled. Neither the Constitution nor the Court can accommodate all sides.

Cases Cited

Beal v. *Doe*, 432 U.S. 438 (1977)
Bellotti v. *Baird*, 443 U.S. 622 (1979)
Cleveland Board of Education v. *LaFleur*, 414 U.S. 632 (1974)
Doe v. *Bolton*, 410 U.S. 179 (1973)
Eisenstadt v. *Baird*, 405 U.S. 438 (1972)
Griswold v. *Connecticut*, 381 U.S. 479 (1965)
H. L. v. *Matheson*, 450 U.S. 398 (1981)
Hammer v. *Dagenhart*, 247 U.S. 251 (1918)
Harris v. *McRae*, 448 U.S. 297 (1980)

Indiana High School Athletic Association v. *Raike*, 329 N.E.2d 66 (1975)

Maher v. *Roe*, 432 U.S. 464 (1977)

Planned Parenthood of Missouri v. *Danforth*, 428 U.S. 52 (1976)

Poelker v. *Doe*, 432 U.S. 519 (1977)

Roe v. *Wade*, 410 U.S. 113 (1973)

Roger H. Davidson

Procedures and Politics in Congress

IF THE Supreme Court justices assumed at the time of *Roe* v. *Wade* that judicial logic would restrict congressional interest in abortion, the assumption was soon shattered. "I am shocked at the ruling," said Senator James Allen at the time of the decision, characterizing it as "bad logic, bad law, and bad morals." Allen reminded his colleagues that thirty-one states' laws were voided by the Court, and that most other states would have to rewrite their laws as a result. On the other side of the Capitol and of the issue, Representative Bella Abzug took the floor to say that "millions of American women feel more secure and more free today as the result of yesterday's Supreme Court ruling."

In the decade following *Roe* v. *Wade*, abortion continued to vex members of Congress, regardless of their approach to the matter. The decision has stimulated a sizable number of legislative efforts to limit or reduce its coverage. According to Congressional Research Service compilations, some thirty statutes enacted between 1973 and 1982 dealt with abortion—all of them involving restrictions of one form or another. The majority were enacted during the 95th and 96th Congresses. Pro-choice lawmakers were on the defensive during this period, fighting to uphold the Supreme Court's formula and to minimize the impact of restrictive proposals. Many more measures were introduced than acted upon. In the 96th Congress alone, for example, seventy-three bills were introduced in the House or Senate containing some type of restrictive abortion provision; fifty-four such measures were introduced in the first eighteen months of the 97th Congress.

Scores of votes in both chambers have been devoted to abortion. The votes reflect fervent lobbying on both sides and the intense views held by segments of the general public. Some 124 national organizations hold positions on abortion rights or have formed specifically to favor or oppose

THIS PAPER reflects the views and conclusions of the author and not those of the Congressional Research Service.

abortion, according to two of the leading federations—the Religious Coalition for Abortion Rights and the National Right to Life Committee. This does not include numerous local organizations, churches, and other groups that have mobilized their members concerning the issue.

Some public opinion surveys have asked whether abortion decisions should be left to the woman and her doctor and whether the Constitution should be amended to make abortion illegal. Three to four times as many respondents avow "strong" views on these questions as profess to hold mild opinions on them.[1] Hence legislators are uncomfortable because they perceive little room for compromise. "I know of no more delicate issue," Senator Robert Dole remarked. "There is no middle ground, where politicians like to be."

Abortion actually spans a range of public policy questions. Legislators' House and Senate floor statements reveal widely diverse attitudes and rationalizations. Even the fight over government-subsidized bans on abortion —by no means the entire range of the problem—embraces foreign policy; the First Amendment (separation of church and state); physician-patient relationships; federal health, environment, and population policies; discrimination and class biases; and health benefit programs for federal employees. Thus the question posed is not always whether legislators approve of abortion or not, but how they approach these other questions.

How can a legislative apparatus cope with a subject that entwines itself around so many tough questions? Ideally, legislative structures and procedures should provide forums for enlightened resolution of such issues. Subject-matter committees should give expert and sustained attention to the details and nuances of policies. The committees should be representative of, and responsive to, the desires of the full chambers. These committees should in turn draw upon research and expert testimony to probe alternative viewpoints and illuminate the consequences of various courses of action. On the floor of both houses, committee experts should explain the background and, if need be, lay out alternatives for final resolution by the full House or Senate. Policy issues and money issues should be treated distinctly but with mutual interdependency. The "rules of the game" should be simple, predictable, and fair to all parties. The policy results should reflect the wishes of the American people—if not their exact views, at least their values and instincts—and should not stray outside the boundaries of their tolerances. In the case of constitutional amendments, the

1. NBC News-Associated Press polls no. 67 (June 4, 1981) and no. 68 (July 24, 1981).

requirements of representativeness are especially rigorous. The legislative action must reflect an overwhelming and enduring public concern.

In reality, the legislative process often strays from these principles. The bulk of policies, it is true, are shaped and refined in the committee and subcommittee rooms of Capitol Hill. However, deliberations often depart from the norm of expert or representative treatment. Committees' members do not always reflect the larger chamber, and not infrequently this results in promoting—or stifling—policy approaches at variance with the wishes of the full chamber. Remedying these deficiencies from the floor of the House or Senate is difficult and clumsy at best, impossible at worst. Lawmaking practices, moreover, tend to yield policies that are drafted and voted on one by one, often with little linkage one to another. Uncoordinated or even inconsistent policies sometimes result. If the choices are linked together, it is typically through implicit or explicit bargains or vote trading.

Nor do votes in the full chamber necessarily yield balanced or even representative judgments. Like all truly intense issues, abortion policy tends to obliterate distinctions among choices faced by legislators. Issues like abortion that are portrayed in absolutist terms tend to break down these compartments. This turns every related issue into an abortion referendum, regardless of competing factors that are in play. Interest groups tend to draw the line between friends and enemies on every vote, regardless of the ambiguities or technicalities. The abortion issue is not alone in this regard; other polarizing issues, like school busing or school prayer, not to mention such historic conflicts as those about slavery, Prohibition, and Communist subversion, evoked similar responses. Such issues, when they come along, blur the usual fragmentation of legislative decisionmaking.

The question is whether efforts in Congress to protect, prohibit, or restrict abortion have been pursued within the broad bounds of the rules of the game or have so stretched the rules as to give cause for concern about the functioning of the legislative process.

Attempts to Prohibit Abortion

While legislative strategies are dictated by political exigencies as well as by the sponsors' goals, most abortion opponents would probably prefer an outright prohibition on abortion other than in a limited number of medically or otherwise compelling cases.

Ever since *Roe* v. *Wade* was handed down in 1973, constitutional amendments have regularly been introduced to overrule the Supreme Court—either directly by extending to fetuses the Fifth and Fourteenth Amendments' guarantees against deprivation of life without due process of law, or indirectly by restoring preexisting state authority to permit or limit abortion. Because the latter approach involves abortion standards that would vary from state to state, the "states' rights" amendment has faded in popularity among abortion foes. Moreover, constitutional amendments come hard. A two-thirds majority in both chambers is required, followed by a long, problematic process of ratification by legislatures or conventions in three-fourths of the states. Close to 10,000 have been proposed, yet only twenty-six enacted.

To avoid the tortuous course of amending the Constitution, proposals have been made to negate *Roe* v. *Wade* by various statutory means. One is a congressional finding of fact that human life begins at conception. Sponsors contend that such a finding would encourage states to enact laws protecting fetuses. Other bills would limit federal court power to deal with abortion. Their underlying assumption is that legislatures would enact prohibitions if freed from the fear of contrary judicial policymaking. And omnibus antiabortion measures include such provisions as those declaring that human life begins at conception, forbidding federal financing of abortion in a variety of contexts, and providing fast-track Supreme Court review of abortion cases.

Whatever their prospects of ultimate passage, before 1981 most of these approaches to banning abortion faced little chance of reaching the House or Senate floor. Just gaining a hearing for such proposals was hard. According to the rules and precedents, all these measures are referred to the Judiciary Committees of the two bodies. In the wake of the civil rights battles of the 1960s, the majority Democrats made certain that members newly assigned to these committees were drawn heavily from the party's liberal ranks. In the 93rd Congress, for example, the House Judiciary Committee ranked second only to the Education and Labor Committee on a liberalism scale. By my calculations, its members reflected an average liberalism score of 55 percent, compared to the House average of 43 percent.[2] Further, with the subcommittee reforms of the early 1970s, liberals captured the chairmanship of several key subcommittees, including those controlling hearings on constitutional amendments. By the 97th Congress, both the House and its Judiciary Committee were more conservative than

2. Adapted from *Congressional Quarterly*'s "Opposition to Conservative Coalition" scores, with the figures recomputed to eliminate the effect of absences from the floor.

they had been a decade earlier, but the committee was still more liberal than the full House. Judiciary members reflected an average liberalism score of 49 percent, 10 points higher than the House average. The liberalism average for committee Democrats was 70 percent, compared to 55 percent for all House Democrats. The Civil and Constitutional Rights Subcommittee, moreover, presented a solid liberal phalanx. And while the correlation is far from perfect between liberalism and tolerance for abortion, it is high enough to help explain why a subject of widespread interest around the country has not been on the House Judiciary Committee agenda since 1976, when it held seven days of hearings. An American Life Lobby legislative consultant called the House Judiciary Committee the most liberal in Congress, and complained that it was out of step:

> Conservatives have gotten little or nothing out of that committee. As the country has moved to the right, the Judiciary Committee has moved even further to the left, if that's possible.[3]

The committee's liberal chairman countered, "On matters pertaining to amendments to the Constitution, you don't proceed very lightly."

The Senate Judiciary Committee has not been as consistently liberal as its House counterpart. Indeed, in the 92nd Congress the committee was slightly less liberal than the chamber as a whole, and its three ranking Democrats were among the chamber's most conservative. By the end of the decade the committee had shifted slightly to the left of the Senate as a whole: its members' average liberalism score was 52 percent, compared to 45 percent for all senators. Like its House counterpart, the liberal majority on the Senate Judiciary Committee showed little disposition to advance the so-called social issues espoused particularly by the conservative coalition. The Subcommittee on Constitutional Amendments held twelve days of hearings on abortion amendments in 1974, but none over the next six years.

In 1981 the victorious Republicans aimed straight for Judiciary. With a 53–47 ratio in the Senate, Republican margins in the committees were narrow. In some instances—such as Labor and Human Resources or Environment and Public Works—the presence of Republican moderates blocked conservative majorities. But Judiciary was a different matter. Spurred by conservatives, the committee's new chairman achieved a conservative majority that included a cluster of newcomers known to be interested in the social issues. The average liberalism score of Judiciary members plunged from 52 percent in 1980 to 37 percent a year later—a shift

3. Gary Curran, quoted in Steven Roberts, "National Mood Helps Shape Congress Committees," *New York Times*, February 15, 1981.

that exceeded the conservative swing in the Senate as a whole; both the Constitution Subcommittee and the Separation of Powers Subcommittee acquired antiabortion chairmen. In addition, conservatives opposed to abortion could expect bonus votes from two Democrats on the committee who on other issues would side with liberals.

Even with control of the subcommittees and the full Senate Judiciary Committee, opponents of abortion did not enjoy easy access to floor consideration during the 97th Congress. First, Republicans agreed to focus on the Reagan economic program during 1981, delaying the contentious social issues until the following year. Although this decision meant further delay in airing these issues on the floor, it provided needed time to hold hearings and develop support. Subsequently, however, a split in the ranks of the antiabortion lobby widened and blunted its impact. The split reflected the two competing approaches to the goal of eliminating abortion—the states' rights amendment versus the statutory route.

Finally, a controversy erupted over hearings on the statutory approach. The subcommittee chairman, a freshman senator, apparently hoped to dispose of the matter in two days of hearings confined to the biological question of when life begins. This hurried schedule, and an initial witness list that was construed as biased, boomeranged as the subcommittee's ranking minority member distributed a three-page letter questioning whether hearings would be scheduled for pro-choice groups. The first day of hearings was marked by outbursts from women opposed to the bill but not scheduled to be heard. Six of the protesters were subsequently arrested for disturbing the proceedings.

A parade of seven witnesses opened the hearings by voicing support for the bill's central thesis that "scientific evidence indicates a significant likelihood that actual human life exists from conception." But the eighth witness, chairman of the Department of Human Genetics at the Yale Medical School, scored the witnesses who preceded him for failing "to distinguish between their moral or religious positions and their professional scientific judgments." "I hope," he said, "that you and the rest of the subcommittee would not take that ratio of 7 to 1 to reflect the scientific opinion of the American scholar. If you wish to know more about how American scientists feel on this issue, I would hope that you will continue to seek additional opinion."[4]

4. Leon E. Rosenberg, in *The Human Life Bill*, Hearings before the Subcommittee on Separation of Powers of the Senate Committee on the Judiciary, 97 Cong. 1 sess. (Government Printing Office, 1982), pp. 51, 60.

To counter charges of biased hearings, the chairman promised "extensive and exhaustive hearings so that all points of view ultimately and finally will have been heard." Conceding further that the issue was a difficult one, he acknowledged that whatever the disposition of the human life bill, "it will not end the debate over abortion. . . . It is a major policy question that will be with us an indefinite period of time. . . . We are not at Armageddon here."[5]

Some abortion opponents were troubled by the hearings for another reason—they feared that the human life statute might derail the progress of a constitutional amendment, believed to be a sounder approach. Indeed, when the subcommittee eventually approved the human life bill on a party line vote, some press accounts found it irresistible to ridicule the 3–2 finding that life begins at conception. Although further action was postponed according to an agreement that the constitutional amendment should be acted upon first, conflicts between the two approaches continued to divide the antiabortion movement.

Charges of undue haste arose again in December 1981, this time ironically in connection with the proposed constitutional amendment giving Congress and the states concurrent authority to restrict abortion. S. Res. 110 was reported from the Constitution Subcommittee following a fifteen-minute markup only one hour after hearings were closed. Declining to vote, a Democratic senator recorded his doubts that the rules of the game were being observed in that "the precedent the subcommittee sets today does material harm to the tradition of public participation in the lawmaking process." The chairman countered that there would be ample time to review the hearings before the full committee took up the measure. After it did so, three months later, the first congressional action directly challenging the Supreme Court's decision emerged from the Senate Judiciary Committee—nine years and two months after *Roe* v. *Wade*. S. Res. 110 was approved by a 10–7 vote following an emotional debate during which one Democrat described his vote as the most difficult one he had cast in the Senate. A Catholic who harbored doubts about imposing "a singular view" on others, he found the issue neither black nor white, but "somewhere in that awful middle." Five conservative Republicans joined him in expressing reservations about the proposed amendment and serving notice that they might try to amend it on the Senate floor.

The narrative above suggests that both sides have committed excesses,

5. Ibid., pp. 37, 38.

but of types not unfamiliar to students of congressional mores. If antiabortion conservatives in the Senate handled the hearing process badly, they also backed off in the face of complaints. If liberal supporters of abortion in the House have blocked hearings on the subject, it should be remembered that most committees fail to act on most measures referred to them. Indeed, it sometimes seems that the major function of committees and subcommittees is to bury bills and resolutions. (Of the nearly 15,000 measures introduced during the 96th Congress, for example, fewer than 2,500 emerged from committee, and only 613 of them actually became public laws.) Extrapolating from statements on the abortion issue, one can conclude that many members believe the Judiciary Committees responded correctly in delaying consideration of antiabortion measures. Some members who personally oppose abortion but are loathe to insert such a provision in the Constitution prefer not to have to vote in the fishbowl of the House or Senate chamber.

As a practical matter, there is little chance of dislodging a measure if a committee refuses to act, but a discharge threat can goad a committee to some action. The House discharge rule is so rarely employed that since 1910, when the rule was adopted, only two discharged measures have ever become law. However, as recently as 1980, a House Judiciary subcommittee held hearings on a school prayer amendment after more than a year's delay. Once pro–school prayer lobbyists persuaded 180 House members to sign the discharge petition, the subcommittee announced hearings, presumably to forestall 38 additional members from signing the petition and forcing a floor vote. There is no way of knowing whether the Judiciary Committee would respond in similar fashion to a comparable show of interest by a significant number of House members.

Curbing Abortion Funding

Affixing floor amendments to committee bills is a tactic for those who have lost out at the committee stage of lawmaking. Amendments to appropriations bills, if they have the effect of altering substantive law, raise troublesome questions of legislative procedure. Amendments to authorizing bills, though procedurally less troublesome, intrinsically challenge the authority of the standing committees. Because committees have been slow to append antiabortion provisions to either regular authorization or appropriations bills, these provisions have taken the form of floor amendments—

often called "Hyde amendments," after their most prominent advocate, Representative Henry J. Hyde.

Such amendments surfaced as early as 1973. That year, without controversy, Congress banned the use of foreign aid funds to perform abortions or coerce anyone into performing them. Added to a federal health bill was a "right of conscience" proviso that protected persons or institutions receiving federal funds against being required to perform abortions in violation of religious or moral beliefs and barred employment discrimination against staff members of such institutions for either performing or refusing to perform abortions because of their convictions.

More recently, provisions limiting abortions have been affixed to a variety of federal programs. Foreign aid authorizations, for example, bar appropriated funds from being used to lobby for abortion and prohibit funding for abortions for Peace Corps volunteers. The 1981 International Security and Development Act forbids using population planning and health program funds to conduct research on abortions or involuntary sterilization as a method of family planning. Abortion restrictions are included in such enactments as the Biomedical Research Act, the Legal Services Corporation Act, and the Nurses Training Act, among others.

Such authorizing provisions do not, however, represent the main battleground for the issue on Capitol Hill. The ultimate goal for *Roe* v. *Wade* opponents is to change the Constitution to bar abortions, or at least restore the local option that prevailed before 1973. Failing that objective, the immediate goal is to stop the use of federal funds to pay for abortions. The prime target has been medicaid, whose recipients are the beneficiaries of the vast majority of federally funded abortions.

The Hyde Amendments

The initial skirmishes over medicaid abortions—in the form of floor amendments to the annual Labor-HEW funding bill—ended inconclusively. The first such amendment, offered late one evening in June 1974 by Representative Angelo Roncallo, would have prohibited federal medicaid financing for any and all abortions. It was rejected by a 123–247 vote. Three months later, a Senate version that prohibited medicaid-financed abortions except when necessary to save the mother's life was adopted by voice vote after a motion to table was soundly defeated, 34–50. But the amendment was dropped by the conference committee with an explanation in its report:

An annual appropriations bill is an improper vehicle for such a controversial and far-reaching legislative provision whose implications and ramifications are not clear, whose constitutionality has been challenged and on which no hearings have been held.[6]

Comparable procedural fastidiousness did not prevail in subsequent confrontations.

After a second failure in 1975—House rejection by voice vote of an amendment barring the use of federal medicaid funds to pay for or encourage abortion—antiabortion forces achieved success in 1976 on their third try. The Hyde amendment was enacted as a rider to the fiscal year 1977 Labor-HEW appropriations bill after a three-month battle over its wording. As Hyde recounted,

[a colleague] got me aside one day and said this bill was coming up that appropriated all sorts of money for abortions, and wouldn't it be a nice idea if we could just sneak an amendment in there that would halt this nefarious practice. We scribbled it out in longhand right on the spot. We waited, and handed it up, and the next thing I knew I was in the well addressing my colleagues on behalf of the right to life.[7]

As originally written, Hyde's amendment would have prohibited any and all medicaid-financed abortions. After eleven weeks and dozens of compromise proposals, the chambers agreed on the following wording: "None of the funds contained in this Act shall be used to perform abortions except where the life of the mother would be endangered if the fetus were carried to term."

The following year saw the bitterest conflict over medicaid-financed abortions. This time the stalemate over Labor-HEW funding lasted five months. The final bill was approved on December 7, after two continuing resolutions expired, and just in time to avoid delaying paychecks to Labor-HEW employees. The House began by voting, 201–155, to substitute a blanket prohibition for the compromise 1976 language. The Senate approved a version allowing abortions if the mother's life were endangered, if rape or incest were involved, or if a physician judged the abortion medically necessary. The House accepted the first two conditions with some modifications; but to many "medically necessary" meant abortion on demand because, it was contended, a physician could always be found to say the procedure was needed. Conferees tried many different wordings, and more

6. H. Rept. 93-1489 in *Congressional Record* (November 21, 1974), p. 36933.

7. Cited in Peg O'Hara, "Congress and the Hyde Amendment . . . How the House Voted to Stop Abortions," *Congressional Quarterly Weekly Report,* vol. 38 (April 19, 1980), p. 1038.

than twenty-five roll-call votes were taken in the two chambers before the final version was accepted. Less restrictive than the 1976 version, the 1977 wording was still vexing to abortion advocates.

After 1977, antiabortion forces continued to register advances. Although Senate strategists succeeded in holding onto the 1977 medicaid language for another year, by 1979 abortion opponents were able to restrict medicaid-financing of abortion except to save the mother's life or in cases of rape or incest, or "where severe and long lasting physical health damage would result if the pregnancy were carried to term." In 1980, the House and Senate deadlocked on the appropriations bill, but a continuing resolution adopted after prolonged debate contained two new wrinkles. First, a rape would have to be reported to police or public health officials within seventy-two hours. Second, states were relieved of any obligation to fund abortions, even those permitted under the Hyde amendment, if they so chose. Even more restrictive provisions—so draconian that not even their supporters described them as "pro-life"—were contained in continuing resolutions approved during the 97th Congress. These allowed abortions only to save the mother's life—no exceptions for rape or incest—and gave states the option of not funding abortions at all.

The various Hyde amendments dramatically slashed federal financing of abortion. In 1976, according to estimates by HEW's Office of Population Affairs, federal expenditures of $45 million to $55 million financed from 250,000 to 300,000 of the approximately 1 million abortions performed. During 1978, according to the department's Office of Policy, Planning, and Research, no more than 2,328 abortions were federally funded, at a cost of $777,158.

Hyde-type amendments have been applied to other forms of governmental aid or services. Since 1979 Congress has barred the Defense Department from paying for abortions. (In 1977 the department funded about 26,500 abortions for military personnel and dependents.) Federal funds appropriated to the District of Columbia may not be spent for abortions, except where the mother's life is endangered or in cases of rape or incest that have been reported promptly. Interest in restricting abortion-related funding remains high. In July 1981 the House passed an amendment prohibiting abortions under federal employees' health plans, except where the mother's life is endangered.

Another proposal would forbid the Legal Services Corporation from providing legal assistance in connection with abortion unless the mother's life was endangered. A rejected amendment would even have barred legal services lawyers from giving legal advice about a client's rights and responsibilities regarding abortion.

In a footnote to the congressional battles, a closely divided Supreme Court upheld the Hyde amendment in a 5–4 decision handed down in July 1980 (*Harris* v. *McRae*). The Court's majority found that the Hyde amendment violated neither the Fifth Amendment's due process or equal protection guarantees nor the First Amendment's establishment of religion clause. The decision did not refer to an *amicus curiae* brief filed by over 200 members of Congress arguing that the congressional funding process should be regarded as a separation of powers issue that the Court should avoid.

The Appropriations Rider Controversy

No fair judgment can be made about whether the Hyde amendments jeopardize accepted legislative procedures without first considering the general problems they illustrate:

1. How much separation can be maintained between authorization and appropriation—that is, between the substance of a law and the provision of funds to implement it?

2. How much deference should the House and Senate show to their standing committees' recommendations: to what extent should members attempt to write legislation on the floor through amendments?

Formal rules of both the House and Senate prohibit "legislation" in general appropriations bills. In the House, "no appropriation shall be reported in any general appropriation bill, or be in order as an amendment thereto, for any expenditure not previously authorized by law" (Rule XXI, clause 2). Senate rules, though less strict, forbid amending general appropriations bills to increase funding or to add a new funding item, "unless it be made to carry out the provisions of some existing law, or treaty stipulation, or act, or resolution previously passed by the Senate during that session" (Rule XVI, paragraph 1). While there are allowable exceptions and a point of order must be raised in timely fashion if either rule is to be enforced, the general thrust of the rules conforms to the textbook view of the legislative process—that is, authorizations must be passed before dollars-and-cents figures are furnished in appropriations bills.

In the House, a legislative rider to an appropriations bill is allowable under the so-called Holman rule if the rider directly reduces expenditures. This rule, initially adopted in 1876, accounts for the bulk of riders attached on the floor by members of the Appropriations Committee. In addition, the House may refuse to appropriate for any program either in whole or in part. That principle of "limitation," although not explicitly authorized by House rules, has been sustained so regularly that it is firmly established. Just as Congress may decline to appropriate for a purpose authorized by law, according to Cannon's Precedents, "so it may by limitation prohibit the use of money for part of the purpose while appropriating for the remainder of it." Such amendments must not impose added duties on executive officers or require judgments or determinations not required by law. This restricts the precision of limitation amendments, as will be seen below. Limitation amendments account for virtually all of the riders added on the House floor by members not on the Appropriations Committee.

The distinction between substantive policy decisions and funding decisions fades away in what Louis Fisher characterizes as "the real world of the legislative process" where "authorization bills contain appropriations, appropriation bills contain authorization, and the order of their enactment is sometimes reversed."[8] It may be that the distinction is conceptually flawed, in that appropriations are in fact policy decisions. And in light of the present congressional budget process, at least as followed since 1980, the distinction has become virtually impossible to maintain.

In practice, it is virtually impossible to tell whether a limitation amendment changes existing law or not. Most limitations probably change at least the intent of existing law. Walter Kravitz concludes that rather than overruling all limitation amendments the chair has developed "distinctions which must be artificial, contrived, and open to varying interpretations." For example, although such amendments cannot impose new duties on executive officials, they may impose "incidental burdens and duties" on them and may indirectly interfere with the discretionary authority of executive officers. Thus the rule and precedents force the chair to exercise personal judgment in interpreting it—a predicament that produces, as Kravitz terms it, "inconsistency and unpredictability in rulings."[9]

Limitation amendments can lead to awkward statutory language. Although the rules and precedents allow a certain amount of policymaking in appropriations bills, such provisions are subject to technical constraints

8. "The Authorization-Appropriation Process in Congress: Formal Rules and Informal Practices," *Catholic University Law Review*, vol. 29 (Fall 1979), pp. 52–53.

9. Walter Kravitz, "Legislation in Appropriation Bills: Procedural Problems in the House of Representatives and Some Options," Congressional Research Service (July 28, 1977), p. 13.

that may affect their form. Especially in the House, members may find themselves voting for policy statements that no one really prefers. The House dispute in 1977 over antiabortion language is a case in point.

The Labor-HEW appropriations bill for fiscal 1978 was reported by the Appropriations Committee with language identical to that of the previous year prohibiting the use of funds "to perform abortions except where the life of the mother would be endangered if the fetus were carried to term." A point of order was raised and sustained against the provision on the grounds that it imposed added duties on the executive branch. (The fact that the same language appeared in the previous year's enactment gave it no immunity to the point of order.)

Representative Hyde then tried another approach that would have barred the use of funds "to pay for abortions or to promote or encourage abortions, except where a physician has certified the abortion is necessary to save the life of the mother." Hyde argued that his amendment imposed new duties only on private physicians, not on executive officials. But a point of order was again sustained on the theory that some of the affected physicians would be federal officials who would be required to make determinations not otherwise required of them by law.

Finally, Hyde offered an amendment barring the use of funds simply "to pay for abortions or to promote or encourage abortions." Hyde explained his dilemma:

> I regret that I must abbreviate this amendment to exclude the therapeutic abortion qualification, the absence of which was raised as a great argument against this amendment when it was offered last session. So it went through with no exceptions whatsoever. And in the conference committee we were able to put in the therapeutic abortion exception where the claim for a life is equal to a claim for a life. But I am forced into this position today by points of order. So be it.[10]

No point of order was raised against this version of the Hyde amendment, which passed handily (201–155), although for both Hyde and his opponents, it was less satisfactory than the more finely tuned versions offered earlier.

The Senate, with its more flexible rules and procedures, coped with a comparable problem by simple floor action. An amendment permitting abortions "where the life of the mother would be endangered," where "medically necessary," or for treatment of rape or incest was challenged by a point of order that the amendment was not germane and that it comprised

10. *Congressional Record* (June 17, 1977), p. 19700.

legislation in an appropriations bill. The Senate itself determines the germaneness of amendments. It found this one germane by a 74–21 vote.

The Hyde amendments and comparable ones restricting federal financing of abortion are all well within the formal and informal rules of both chambers. Many appropriations riders are controversial and efforts are periodically launched to curtail or eliminate them, but neither House nor Senate has done so. As long ago as 1946, the Joint Committee on the Organization of Congress proposed that the rules be "tightened effectively" to halt legislation in appropriations bills—a practice the Joint Committee called "often destructive of orderly procedure." The committee argued that: (1) riders "obstruct and retard" the debate on funding measures; (2) they sometimes cost more to implement than the purported savings; and (3) they sometimes contradict action earlier approved in "carefully considered legislation." This last consideration no doubt underlay the thinking of the panel, which noted that without reform "the regular jurisdiction of the standing committees of the House and the Senate will continue to be impinged upon by the appropriating committees."

In the wake of the controversy over the Hyde amendments, the liberal House Democratic Study Group examined appropriations riders in a 1978 report that evaluated various reforms: (1) prohibit all appropriations riders; (2) prohibit floor amendment riders only; (3) prohibit riders unless directed by the authorizing committee; (4) require a two-thirds vote for approval; and (5) deal with riders on an ad hoc basis in the Rules Committee. The House chose none of the above. But one resolution proposing to bar limitation amendments altogether and drop the Holman rule drew twenty-four cosponsors, most of them liberals. If abortion controversy was not the sole reason for this proposal, it was undoubtedly a prime factor. In 1977 the principal sponsor reminded his colleagues, "We underwent a tortuous and protracted experience attempting to resolve the 'Hyde amendment' with eleven votes in the House and a total of twenty-eight votes in both houses." But the resolution died.

By the time of the Democratic Study Group report, appropriations riders (most of them limitation amendments) had become increasingly common on the House and Senate floors. Moreover, such amendments were more likely to succeed. Whereas few limitation amendments were adopted before 1970, at least half of such amendments proposed were adopted in each year between 1977 and 1980. Changes in voting procedures and reduced deference to standing committees mean that more business generally is now conducted via floor amendment than used to be the case. There are also partisan or factional facets of this phenomenon: during the Kennedy-Johnson era, most limitation amendments were sponsored by Republicans, and during the Nixon-Ford years, most were offered by Democrats. Recently, however, as floor amendments have become more common, sponsorship seems more equally divided.

Underlying members' ambivalence about changing these procedures despite their awkwardness and potential for disorder is the use made of them at one time or another by virtually all members and factions. If conservatives used the device in the late 1970s to pass antiabortion limitations (not to mention provisions on busing, school prayers, bilingual education, and the like), liberals used riders in the early 1970s to choke off funds for military operations in Southeast Asia. Limitation amendments were the only way of ending financing for the supersonic transport. Such amendments have also proved useful to members in limiting water projects, occupational health and safety regulations, aid to Angola or Mozambique, salary increases for members of Congress, agricultural price supports, and ship construction in foreign shipyards. Whether appropriations riders that restrict federal financing of abortion are wise or unwise policy is debatable. That such riders are entirely legitimate, even routine, procedural devices is beyond question.

Conclusions

For the legislative process in Congress, the abortion controversy poses hard questions relating to the metes and bounds of power and to the clarity of rules and procedures. Among these issues are the power of committees to bottle up issues, the fairness of committee hearings and markups, the propriety of legislatively altering courts' jurisdiction, the proper subjects for constitutional amendments, and the degree of separation between authorization and appropriation.

While there has been no gross distortion of the system, legislative processes have not done justice to the gravity and complexity of abortion as a public policy problem. Few committee hearings have been held; when they were, questions of fairness were frequently raised. There has been little real committee deliberation upon the issue: with battle lines clearly drawn, there was little tolerance for fine-tuning the provisions or evaluating the options. Actual floor debate, though heated, has been surprisingly brief. Even during the 1982 Senate filibuster on abortion, sometimes there was no senator who wished to speak. At the same time, many hours have been devoted to seemingly endless floor votes on abortion language. The provisions emerging from such stalemates are—according to supporters and opponents alike—clumsy and unsatisfactory.

Behind these workings of rules and procedures is the bitter and uncompromising politics of abortion. Intensely held views like those on either side of the abortion issue inevitably find expression in legislative behavior designed to exploit rules to the fullest, even to bend them to affect the results. Political motivations have the habit of overrunning structural boundaries and procedural distinctions. That this occurs is perhaps deplorable or in some sense dysfunctional. To say that it is hardly surprising is not to say that congressional actions on abortion are correct or wise. It is only to repeat the axiom that passion and procedure are often at odds; whichever prevails, the other is bound to suffer.

G. Calvin Mackenzie

A Test of Fitness
for Presidential Appointment?

INFLUENCE in the appointment of public officials may be as effective an entry to control of public policy as influence in the electoral or legislative processes. The shape of policy reflects the concerns and biases of those appointed to high office as well as those elected. The importance of appointed officers is acknowledged in the Constitution, which requires the advice and consent of the Senate in the appointment of nearly all policy-making officials of the federal government. Consequently, two points of access in the appointment process—the president's designation of a nominee and the Senate's confirmation of that nominee's appointment—provide opportunities for those who want to see their policy concerns reflected in the selection of personnel. Americans have been trying to take advantage of those opportunities since the administration of George Washington. Whether and how they are doing so in connection with the abortion dispute deserve examination in an inquiry into the consequences of the dispute for the governmental system.

A question that has long troubled participants in, and students of, the appointment process can be put in simple terms: What constitutes fitness for office? Is it merely competence, integrity, and good moral character? Or is it also possession of a political philosophy and a set of policy views that concur broadly with those of the people who will pass formal judgment on the nomination?

The Founding Fathers gave only passing attention to this question. They left no answer and few clues. In the ensuing two centuries, judges, scholars, and constitutional lawyers have built arguments all around the question but have failed to find any common ground. Hence we have no legal guidance to the kinds of criteria that may appropriately be applied in determining whether an individual is qualified and fit for appointment to a position of responsibility in the federal government.

But if constitutional theory and legal debate have yielded no consensus

47

on the determinants of "fitness," two centuries of political practice have. Given the absence of compelling requirements to do otherwise, the politicians who have controlled the appointment process have shown little reluctance to treat policy considerations—including the policy preferences and personal opinions of potential appointees—as perfectly acceptable tests of fitness to serve. An early, important example is the outcome of Washington's nomination in 1795 of John Rutledge of South Carolina to be chief justice of the United States. Rutledge was a jurist of some eminence, having served previously as an associate justice of the U.S. Supreme Court and as chief justice of the South Carolina Supreme Court. But Rutledge's nomination was not well received by the Senate. Shortly before Washington selected him, he made a speech in Charleston strongly denouncing the Jay treaty with Great Britain, which the Federalist-dominated Senate had just ratified. In anger over this, the Senate rejected Rutledge's appointment by a vote of 14 to 10. Thomas Jefferson noted the significance of this action when he wrote, "The rejection of Mr. Rutledge by the Senate is a bold thing, because they cannot pretend any objection to him but his disapprobation of the treaty." This was the first instance in which a presidential appointment failed because of the nominee's policy views. It would not be the last.

While participants in the appointment process have often declared themselves concerned only with the competence and integrity—and not with the political philosophy—of presidential appointees, their declarations have tended to be little more than lip service. Few of them have observed those restrictions when forced to decide on a candidate whose views on important policy issues were different from their own. The historical record implies quite clearly that personal policy views are widely accepted as an appropriate test of fitness for appointment to high office. Nothing in the recent appointment controversies where abortion was an issue suggests that a change is at hand.

The Record to Date

The pace of public concern with the abortion issue began to quicken in the 1960s and rose to a crescendo with the Supreme Court's watershed decision in 1973. Yet it has only been since the 1976 election that the issue has begun to have an effect on the appointment process. When F. David Mathews was nominated in 1975 to be secretary of health, education, and welfare, the government agency with the principal jurisdiction over abortion policy, the Ford administration did not inquire in advance about his personal views on abortion, nor was he asked to express those views in his Senate confirmation hearing. When John Paul Stevens was nominated to fill the first vacancy to occur on the Supreme Court after its controversial 1973 abortion rulings, he was not asked a single question about his views on abortion in his confirmation hearings.

The inattention to the abortion issue in the selection and confirmation of these two major appointees was characteristic of the hands-off attitude that predominated in the Ford administration and Congress. The Senate at the time was controlled by a pro-choice majority that was largely satisfied with the federal policies established by *Roe* v. *Wade.* Because President Ford was not sending up nominations of vigorous pro-life advocates, the Senate felt no need to use its confirmation authority to affect abortion policy.

Things began to change slowly after the 1976 election. Jimmy Carter was the first elected president to have provided the voters with a clear expression of his personal views on abortion. One might have anticipated an effort by Carter and his staff to select appointees who shared his views and would use their administrative and judicial discretion to bring federal abortion policy into line with the president's views. The nomination of Joseph A. Califano, Jr., as Carter's HEW secretary seemed to signal that determination since, as Califano indicated at his confirmation hearings, he and the president were of like mind on the abortion issue:

> My own personal view, which is the same as Governor Carter's—and we come to the the problem from entirely different cultural, social, and religious backgrounds—is as follows. . . .
>
> That abortion is wrong, that Federal funds should not be used for abortion, but that alternatives should be sought vigorously to prevent abortion situations —alternatives ranging from improving our programs for teenage pregnancies, to foster care, to day-care, family planning, a broad sex education, improved and facilitated adoption procedures and what have you.[1]

Shortly after his election, however, Carter made a decision that effectively undercut any attempt he might have made to ensure the appointment of people who shared his abortion views. He decided to decentralize the selection process, delegating control over subcabinet personnel selection to individual cabinet secretaries. In HEW, where Secretary Califano was overseeing the selection of his own team, principal emphasis was on mana-

---

1. *Hearings on the Nomination of Joseph A. Califano, Jr. to be Secretary of Health, Education, and Welfare*, Hearings before the Senate Committee on Labor, 95 Cong. 1 sess. (Government Printing Office, 1977), p. 14.

gerial skills and policy expertise. Adherence to any specific position on abortion was not a significant selection criterion.

Califano did face some close questioning on abortion during his confirmation hearings before the Senate Committee on Labor and Public Welfare. Indeed these were the first confirmation hearings in which abortion emerged as a significant matter of discussion. Califano's opposition to abortion was well known, and several committee members were concerned lest his strong personal views interfere with his ability to fully enforce the federal abortion laws. Senator William Hathaway put the matter this way:

> I am not so sure that we as individual Members of Government, whether we are in the administration or in the Congress, should be forcing our religious or other beliefs of this nature upon the public in general. . . .
>
> It seems to me that this particular belief falls into this category. Therefore, although we respect your right to hold it, we think—at least some of us think— that it should not be implemented in your policies, should not cause you to campaign against Federal funding. Because in this case being against Federal funding, it seems to me, is to say that the Federal Government should prohibit those who are totally dependent upon Federal funding for medical care from ever getting abortions, even though the Supreme Court has guaranteed them that right as private citizens under certain circumstances.[2]

Also appearing to testify at the Califano hearings was a representative of the National Abortion Rights Action League, a pro-choice interest group. The group did not directly oppose the Califano appointment, but it did ask that the confirmation hearings be used to require Califano to separate his own beliefs from the existing government policy of providing medicaid reimbursement for abortions. "It would be deeply disturbing," the group contended, "to see a Secretary attempt to undermine or restrict current policy solely upon the basis of moral and religious beliefs not shared by the majority of the American public."[3]

The Califano appointment was not rejected or even seriously jeopardized because of Califano's abortion views. His appointment was confirmed overwhelmingly. What is significant is that the confirmation process was used by people concerned about Califano's abortion views, first, as a mechanism for exploring those views carefully and publicly, and, second, as an opportunity to sensitize him to his responsibility to enforce the law regardless of his feelings about its propriety.

With the exception of the Califano appointment, the abortion issue played little part in appointment decisions through the rest of the Carter

2. Ibid., p. 47.
3. Ibid., p. 68.

administration. This reflects both the lack of interest of the administration in using its appointment powers to shape a specific abortion policy and the precarious balance that existed in the Senate by then between the pro-life and pro-choice forces. Had one been making an assessment early in 1980, the temptation would have been strong to argue that the effect of the abortion issue on the appointment process fell somewhere between minimal and nonexistent.

That notion was set aside rather quickly by the election of 1980, which produced both a president more firmly opposed than any of his predecessors to the legalization of abortion and a Senate controlled by a pro-life majority. The impact on the appointment process was immediate and potentially far-reaching.

Ronald Reagan, more than any of the postwar presidents, intended to use his appointment powers to impress his own views on public policy. Reagan was determined to appoint people who shared his political philosophy about abortion, as well as other policy areas, and who would use their authority aggressively to move government policy in the directions that he desired.

Reagan's choice for secretary of health and human services was Senator Richard S. Schweiker, a constant supporter of abortion restrictions in the Senate. To lead the Office of Adolescent Pregnancy Programs in HHS, Reagan appointed Marjory Mecklenburg, who had been active in the anti-abortion movement, serving most recently as president of the American Citizens Concerned for Life. Reagan's nominee for the position of surgeon general and head of the Public Health Service was C. Everett Koop, a Philadelphia pediatrician, who was older than the mandatory retirement age for the post, had never served in the Public Health Service (as required by law), and had no substantial training in public health or preventive medicine. Koop was, however, a vigorous pro-life advocate who had traveled widely around the country lecturing against abortion.

The growing salience of the abortion issue also became more apparent in confirmation proceedings after 1980. While the Senate granted its traditional deference to a new president in staffing his own administration, the abortion issue did emerge prominently in the Koop hearings. Koop was confirmed after a set of intricate legislative maneuverings in which his opponents tried first to prevent the lifting of the statutory restrictions on his nomination and then to defeat the appointment itself.

The Koop confirmation demonstrated the polarization that can result from the nomination of someone who holds absolutist views on abortion.

There was no question where Koop stood. His position was so clear and his commitment to it so tenacious that his opponents could find no common ground with him. Given the visibility of abortion in this proceeding, many senators felt they had to base their confirmation vote on that issue. Twenty-four of them voted against Everett Koop.

This was an unusually clear case of an appointment decided solely on the basis of numerical strength. Over the years the confirmation process has often been used as a mechanism for narrowing or resolving conflicts between presidential appointees and individual senators. Recent history is replete with examples of this interaction. When Richard Nixon nominated Walter Hickel to be secretary of the interior in 1968, Hickel made some unfortunate remarks that appeared to jeopardize his chances of confirmation. He said that he did not believe in "conservation for conservation's sake" and that he could "do more for Alaska as secretary of interior than he could as governor of Alaska." His confirmation hearing, however, permitted members of the Senate Interior Committee to explore Hickel's views in depth and to satisfy themselves that his approach to the Interior job was more acceptable to them than they might have surmised from the reports they had read in the press.

When Robert H. McKinney was nominated by Jimmy Carter to serve as head of the Federal Home Loan Bank Board, he was the target of opposition from people who disliked what they perceived to be his views on the regulation of the savings and loan industry. Consumer groups especially could not believe that McKinney, the chairman of a savings and loan bank, would be an effective regulator of the industry from which he came. Several of these groups testified against his appointment. Some members of the Senate Banking Committee also raised serious doubts about his likely objectivity. But again the confirmation hearings permitted a mutual exploration of ideas and concerns and gave McKinney an opportunity to convince the Banking Committee that he could be an aggressive and objective regulator despite his experience in the savings and loan industry. He might not have been approved by the committee had a vote been taken before the hearing; his nomination was approved overwhelmingly afterward.

These illustrations identify an important characteristic of the confirmation process. It allows presidential appointees and individual senators to discuss their personal differences freely and to look for areas of agreement and common purpose. That has been one of the significant contributions of the confirmation process to American public administration: fostering communication and mutual understanding between the legislative and executive branches. But when policy views are as divergent and unyielding as they were on the abortion issue in the Koop case, the confirmation process serves no such purpose. It becomes instead a show of strength. A nominee may be confirmed, as Koop was, but he begins his appointment in an atmosphere of bitterness and distrust that can only impede the effectiveness of his public service.

Another indication of the possible future impact of the abortion issue on the appointment process occurred with the nomination of Sandra Day O'Connor to the Supreme Court. As a member of the Arizona legislature before her appointment to the bench, she had cast votes on several bills that involved the abortion issue. On a few of those occasions she had voted against an absolute pro-life position, usually for procedural reasons. In 1974, for instance, she had voted against an amendment to a bill allowing the University of Arizona to issue bonds to expand its football stadium. The amendment would have prohibited the performance of abortions in any facility under the jurisdiction of the Arizona Board of Regents. She indicated that her opposition to the amendment had nothing to do with her views on abortion, but rather reflected her concern, as the Senate majority leader, with the attachment of nongermane riders to Senate bills.

Abortion was the only truly contentious issue at the O'Connor confirmation hearings. During the hearings, antiabortion groups maintained picket lines outside the Dirksen Senate Office Building. Their concern, like that of pro-life senators, was that the appointment of anyone other than an antiabortion absolutist would only prolong the moderate Supreme Court majority on this issue and thus postpone the reversal of *Roe* v. *Wade.*

At the outset of her confirmation hearing, Judge O'Connor sought to clarify her personal views on abortion:

[Abortion] is simply offensive to me. It is . . . repugnant to me and something in which I would not engage.

I am opposed to it as a matter of birth control or otherwise. The subject of abortion is a valid one, in my view, for legislative action subject to any constitutional restraints or limitations.[4]

She also qualified her discussion of the issue by indicating her belief that

the personal views and philosophies . . . of a Supreme Court Justice and indeed any judge should be set aside insofar as it is possible to do that in resolving matters that come before the Court.

Issues that come before the Court should be resolved based on the facts of that

4. *Hearings on the Nomination of Sandra Day O'Connor to be Associate Justice of the U. S. Supreme Court,* Hearings before the Senate Committee on the Judiciary, 97 Cong. 1 sess. (GPO, 1981), pp. 61, 125.

particular case or matter and on the law applicable to those facts, and any constitutional principles applicable to those facts. They should not be based on the personal views and ideology of the judge with regard to that particular matter or issue.[5]

None of this deterred those who questioned the depth and conviction of her opposition to abortion. Senators Jeremiah A. Denton, Jr., and John P. East led the questioning on this issue, with Denton arguing that abortion was the critical issue in the confirmation decision:

> Granting that abortion is a single issue, but counting it fundamental to our democratic form of Government, I regard legalized abortion as a denial of the most fundamental and efficacious national principle of the Nation. My judgment on voting on your confirmation or on the confirmation of any other nominee—male or female—to the Supreme Court will be affected by that belief of mine.[6]

Pro-life senators sought throughout the hearings to get O'Connor to address the *Roe* v. *Wade* decision and to express her views on it. This she steadfastly declined to do, indicating her belief that the issue might well return to the Court in the near future and that she should not make any prejudgment. This was in line with the caution of previous Supreme Court nominees at their confirmation hearings, but it hardly satisfied the curiosity and concern of the pro-life faction on the Judiciary Committee. However, the Senate unanimously confirmed O'Connor's nomination.

One might draw several conclusions from the events surrounding the O'Connor appointment. One is, of course, that deference to a president's nominee remains a very strong controlling force in the confirmation process. Without clear evidence of personal indiscretion or incompetence, those who wish to defeat a nominee will continue to have their work cut out for them.

This appointment also seems to suggest a growing commitment on the part of pro-life senators to use the leverage afforded them by the confirmation process to try to change federal abortion policy. O'Connor had impeccable conservative credentials and, on the issue of abortion, her personal views and her political record put her very close to the strongest of the antiabortion advocates. Yet for the antiabortion interest groups and a number of antiabortion senators, that was not good enough. Any position that fell short of the philosophical purity they expected was not acceptable on this issue.

Equally noteworthy in this case was the admission of some of

5. Ibid., p. 60.
6. Ibid., p. 28.

O'Connor's Senate questioners that they were willing to let their vote on her confirmation turn on this single issue. This represents a considerable break with the conventional Senate rhetoric that a confirmation judgment should be based on a comprehensive evaluation of a president's nominee. While senators have occasionally wavered from that sentiment in practice, they have adhered to it closely in public descriptions of their responsibilities.

The abortion controversies that have arisen in the appointment process in the 1980s suggest a growing absence of moderation. Where the issue is relevant, pro-life advocates appear willing to support nominees who take an absolutist position against abortion and to challenge nominees whose position is not in complete concurrence with their own. Pro-choice advocates appear to be similarly firm in their opposition to nominees with strong antiabortion views.

Caution is appropriate in making this assessment. The recent evidence is limited to a few cases. It is not yet certain whether the actions and attitudes that emerged in the Koop and O'Connor appointments are anomalous or whether they indicate the establishment of a pattern in appointments in which abortion is a major concern. One can only conclude that the abortion issue has had a limited effect on the appointment process to date, but there is also ample support for the suspicion that the battle lines are beginning to harden on this issue and that the appointment process could well become one of the important grounds on which the battle over abortion policy is fought. That occurrence will not be without significant implications for abortion policy—or for the appointment process itself.

Making the Future Work

Despite their dismay at the Supreme Court's decision in *Roe* v. *Wade* and despite the fact that public opinion polls consistently find them in the minority, for those Americans who are opposed to legalized abortion, the last decade has been one of substantial success. Abortion opponents are better organized and better financed now than they have ever been. They are perceived by some politicians to be a potent force in electoral politics. They have succeeded in restricting the use of federal funds to pay for abortions for the poor and for federal dependents. And efforts have been launched to prevent the use of employee health insurance benefits to pay for abortions and to restrict federal legal aid agencies from litigating abortion cases.

Taken collectively, this represents a broad and increasingly successful effort by antiabortion groups to pursue every available opportunity to narrow federal support for legalized abortion. The evidence cited earlier suggests that the appointment process is also beginning to be used for that same purpose. That seems apparent in President Reagan's conscious selection of vigorous pro-life advocates to relevant positions in the Department of Health and Human Services. And it seems as well to characterize the response to several of Reagan's nominations by senators on both sides of the abortion issue. If, indeed, the appointment process is to be used more frequently as a fulcrum for those trying to alter the balance of federal abortion policy, some heed must be paid to the meaning and the likely consequences of that use.

First, is the appointment process an appropriate forum for this debate over abortion policy? Should the appointment process be confined to examinations of the character, competence, and integrity of candidates for positions in the executive and judicial branches, or should policy considerations be permitted to play a major role in the selection and confirmation of those candidates?

There are no simple answers to this question. To suggest, for instance, that candidates' personal views on abortion are not an appropriate factor in considering their fitness for appointment is little more than whistling into the wind. As indicated earlier, the appointment process has always served as a kind of policy subsystem: a side channel perhaps, but one in which the future shape of public policy has always been a central and accepted consideration. This is no less true now than it has ever been.

Presidents believe that the kind of people they appoint affects the kind of policy the government produces. Senators agree. Presidents thus shape the selection process to fit their needs as they define them. The Senate shapes the confirmation process to fit its needs as it defines them. There is no effective way to stop them from doing what they think is right and necessary. Similarly, if either side in the abortion dispute thinks there is advantage to be gained by injecting its own views into appointment decisions, it will do just that.

It is simplistic to suggest, however, that a philosophy of "anything goes" is the proper approach here, that the appointment process is flexible and sinewy enough to tolerate any kind of controversy. This misapprehends the fragile political nature of the process. There is nothing action-forcing about it; stalemate is always a possible outcome. If presidents and senators and other political actors insist on making this a battleground of the abortion controversy, there should be no surprise at long delays in filling executive and judicial positions that become the focus of that debate, or at an increase in the number of appointees wounded by bruising confirmation fights whose effectiveness in office is subsequently impaired.

The politics of abortion seem to run against the grain of the traditional politics of the appointment process. The latter requires cooperative interaction among a wide range of individuals. It is a politics of coalition building in which agreement on appointments evolves from the negotiated settlement of clashing perspectives. Abortion politics, however, defy successful coalition building. Though belief on the issue is not unconditional, on the fundamental question of whether a woman has *any* right to an abortion there are two opposite and mutually exclusive positions. Hence delay, stalemate, and bitter acrimony become likely outcomes of appointment disputes.

That those controversies will continue to arise in the appointment process seems unavoidable. The absolutists on one side believe that abortion is murder. The absolutists on the other believe that a woman's right to an abortion is undeniable. And because an appointee must either oppose abortion absolutely or think it permissible under some conditions, one could expect activists on this issue—both inside and outside the government—to work for the nomination and confirmation of appointees whose abortion views align with their own.

Since it is likely that the abortion issue will come to play a growing role in the appointment process, what can be done to prepare for that development? The core of the task is to determine how the appointment process can best serve the needs of advocates on both sides of the issue without itself breaking down. How can the politics and the formal operations of the appointment process simultaneously assist in the conduct of the abortion debate and preserve the integrity of the process itself? That is the critical question.

The ability of the appointment process to tolerate the strains it will incur as it becomes a forum for vigorous debate depends on two things. The first is that the participants in that debate understand the purposes and the parameters of the appointment process and are sensitive to the ways in which appointment decisions can affect public policy, especially on the issue of abortion. The second is that they be willing to adhere to a few simple ground rules that need not obstruct consideration of appointees' abortion views, but should hold that consideration within the narrow bounds of relevance.

Critical to the maintenance of the appointment process is the understanding that it is just that: a process. It is not merely a lonesome decision made by a president, nor simply a vote cast by a Senate committee. A decision on an appointment is instead a series of steps in which a number of political actors are able to participate influentially. If their concern is with the impact of a personnel choice on public policy—and that has always been the driving concern in the appointment process—they have a number of ways to shape that impact. Outright rejection is not the only option for those who have qualms about an appointee's views.

Over the years, the Senate has developed a number of techniques for controlling a nominee's actions in office. Senate committees use confirmation hearings to communicate their policy intentions and objectives to the nominee. The latter's policy views are often explored in depth, especially by those senators who disagree with them. When the disagreement is relevant and substantial, committees often require nominees to make a public pledge to take or not take certain actions while in office. The confirmation of Elliot Richardson's appointment as attorney general in 1973 was delayed, for instance, until Richardson named a Watergate special prosecutor and pledged to support the prosecutor's independence. When President Nixon later ordered Richardson to fire the special prosecutor, Richardson felt that his pledge to the Senate Judiciary Committee prevented him from doing that and so he resigned from office.

Not always content to rely on the honor of nominees for the maintenance of pledges made during confirmation hearings, Senate committees often use other devices. One is to require the appointee to submit a report indicating the manner in which he has conformed to pledges made in confirmation hearings. For example, General William McKee, who became head of the Federal Aviation Administration during the Johnson administration, was required to report to the Commerce Committee every time a civilian employee was replaced by a member of the armed forces.

Vigilance by senators and committee staff members is the most important way in which pledges are enforced. A violated pledge often results in a strongly worded admonition to the appointee involved. In his confirmation hearings, for instance, John H. Reed promised the Commerce Committee that he would strive to prevent political interference in the deliberations of the National Transportation Safety Board, which he was to head. When it was revealed two years later that the board had withheld a report because it was critical of the Nixon administration, Reed received a written rebuke from Senator Warren Magnuson, the chairman of the Commerce Committee, and a demand that he provide complete information on the incident to the committee.

Pledges of this sort are commonly elicited as a condition of confirmation. When a nominee is reluctant to agree to restraints in this fashion, it is not uncommon for committees to delay action on his confirmation until the nominee accedes to the committee's demands.

Because of these different ways in which senators can limit an appointee's influence on public policy, the confirmation power need not be used simply as a blunt instrument. The range of opportunities for influence is wider and more subtle than a mere up-or-down vote on a nomination. And this range of available techniques provides a greater capacity for conflict containment than a hasty glance at the appointment process might suggest.

An awareness of these opportunities should help to prevent advocates on either side of the abortion issue from "going to the mat" whenever they confront an appointee whose views they dislike. There is no absolute necessity under the American system to fully and finally resolve value conflicts whenever they emerge. What is necessary, however, is to provide peaceful arenas for the articulation of these conflicts and for the constant renewal of efforts to balance them within the law. If its character and possibilities are understood by those who participate in it, the appointment process can be one such arena.

Equally critical to the preservation of the appointment process is the understanding that it affords, at best, limited scope for shaping federal abortion policy. In some substantive areas, appointees have broad discretion to shape policy within their jurisdiction. In agencies that award federal grants-in-aid, in regulatory commissions, and at the Federal Reserve Board, to name just a few, policy directions are strongly sensitive to the ideas and objectives of the people in charge. In the court system, and especially on the Supreme Court, there is a constant flow of evidence supporting the old notion that "the law is what the judges say it is." But the impact of government personnel on policy is not consistent: it is directly proportional to the ambiguity of policy in a particular substantive area. Where policy is clearly and comprehensively defined in basic law, discretion is minimal; where policy is loosely defined, discretion is substantial. I would maintain that abortion policy tends to fall into the former category.

The basic "law" on federal abortion policy is *Roe* v. *Wade*, which establishes a woman's right to an abortion and lays out the conditions under which that right can be exercised. Congress has taken several statutory actions since *Roe* v. *Wade* to limit the use of federal funds to pay for legal abortions. In so doing, it has used increasingly specific language in directing how those statutes are to be implemented. One of its purposes in acting this way was to remove whatever discretion it could from the hands of administrators.

The result is that federal abortion policies are about as unambiguous as a policy can be. Little latitude is left to administrators in interpreting these policies. That means, of course, that attempts to use the appointment process to affect abortion policy are unlikely to provide much leverage to those who feel strongly about abortion. If there is leverage to be gained in this process, it is likely to have effect only at the very periphery of abortion policy. The core of that policy, its central thrust, has been well fortified against the whims and personal biases of federal administrators.

There is one notable exception to this lack of leverage, and that is appointments to the Supreme Court. The Supreme Court is the principal creator of current federal abortion policy, and it has the authority and the ability to undo in the future what it has done in the past. Hence, for those concerned with abortion policy, appointments to the Supreme Court will remain a matter of great interest. But the appointment process will be best served if advocates on either side of this issue recognize that other appointments, even those in the area of health and contraception policy, cannot have much influence over the shape of abortion policy and are probably not worth a fight that could harm the long-term ability of the government to staff these positions. An understanding of the limited opportunities for influencing abortion policy afforded by the appointment process and a due sense of proportion on the part of those seeking such influence will do much to maintain the effectiveness of the appointment process.

The history of the appointment process suggests two simple ground rules, long observed in practice, that ought to guide the efforts of pro-life and pro-choice advocates in using the appointment process to pursue their policy objectives. Recognition of, and a willingness to adhere to, these ground rules is the best hope, not only for continued effectiveness of the appointment process, but also for it to contribute to the reasonable conduct of the national debate over abortion policy.

Rule 1 is that an appointee's personal views on abortion, while an appropriate topic of examination, should be a significant factor in selection and confirmation decisions only if he or she is being considered for a position that has some jurisdiction over abortion policy. Even the most vigorous advocates on each side of the abortion issue have admitted that it is an issue on which honorable men and women can disagree. It is not an issue like racial discrimination, where national values and government policy lean so heavily in one direction as to justify efforts to keep from any office those who don't share the prevailing values. One could argue persuasively, for instance, that no racist or anti-Semite should receive any federal appointment, but a similar argument is difficult to construct for pro-life or pro-choice advocates on the issue of abortion. National sentiment is intensely divided; value conflicts cut several different ways. It is hard to find much to be gained by making abortion views an applicable criterion in determining a person's fitness to hold a position having no jurisdiction over abortion policy. Following this first rule is an important way to constrain the potentially harmful effects of the abortion debate on the appointment process. To do otherwise will not only aggravate conflict unnecessarily, but will also deprive the government of the services of highly qualified people whose views on abortion—however irrelevant they may be to the position under consideration—are unacceptable to the president or to some members of the Senate. Enticing qualified citizens to enter high-level government service is difficult enough without adding this further, needless burden.

Rule 1 raises a question about where the line should be drawn between those positions that have jurisdiction over abortion policy and those that do not. Some cases are relatively simple; others are not. The case can be made, for instance, that the abortion views of a nominee to be assistant secretary of HHS for human development services, among whose responsibilities are a number of family planning activities, are an appropriate topic for examination. The same case cannot be made for a nominee to head the Geological Survey. That distinction is not difficult.

Difficulty does arise, however, in those gray areas where a particular position *might* have some jurisdiction over abortion policy under some circumstance. The assistant secretary of defense for health affairs may be responsible for policy decisions that determine the conditions under which government-financed abortions will be provided for female soldiers and dependents. The director of the Office of Personnel Management may well participate in policy decisions about the use of federal employee health insurance benefits to pay for abortions. Should the abortion views of these nominees be a significant factor in their selection and confirmation? That is harder to say. Because participants in an appointment decision cannot be denied the right to raise whatever issues they think are relevant, abortion may become a factor even where it represents only a very small part of a nominee's future responsibilities. A reasonable treatment of abortion considerations in these gray areas may well depend, therefore, on the willingness of the involved parties to abide by Rule 2.

Rule 2 holds that even when a position does involve jurisdiction over abortion policy, participants in the appointment process have a responsibility to consider more than just the appointee's personal views on abortion. These views ought to be weighed among a number of factors, the relative weight varying perhaps with the extent to which abortion policy will require the appointee's attention once in office.

The reasoning behind this rule should be clear to those on both sides of the abortion issue. The "right" views on this issue do not in themselves qualify an individual for any federal office if he or she does not also satisfy fundamental standards of integrity, competence, and character. Even those who agree with a candidate's abortion views will not be well served if that candidate lacks the capacity to translate those views into public policy. On the other hand, the "wrong" views should not automatically disqualify an individual who has other compensating virtues or qualifications, especially if abortion policy is not a central concern of the office in question.

Government is a hard business. Its successful administration requires the appointment of people with a range of talent, sensitivity, and experience that is precious and uncommon. Possession of a single set of policy views cannot compensate for the absence of those qualities; no policy objectives can be effectively pursued without them. No single ideological litmus test can possibly guarantee the kind of responsive and creative leadership that effective public service requires.

Conclusion

There is nothing quite so intellectually dangerous as trying to plot a response to the future before the future reveals itself. It is uncertain how large and consequential a role abortion will come to play in the appointment process. To date, its impact has been limited to a few notable but not unmanageable appointment controversies. That may be all one can expect in the future.

But that seems unlikely. The abortion issue has become increasingly prominent in national politics. Advocates on both sides have broadened their search for avenues of influence. The appointment process has come to be recognized as one of those. The likelihood is that more people will attempt to exploit it to their advantage as time passes.

If that occurs—and one can reasonably expect that it will—the future effectiveness of the appointment process may be jeopardized by contention over nominees' views on abortion. The primary jeopardy is that agreement on appointments may become so elusive that administrative and judicial positions may remain vacant for long periods, or that those who survive the appointment process and fill them may be so wounded by the effects of that process as to be unable to perform effectively in office. The double jeopardy is that talented people may be reluctant to depart the security of the private sector for public service, knowing that their personal views on abortion may be the subject of intense scrutiny and attack in the appointment process.

Nothing recounted or proposed here will guarantee that reason will prevail over emotion, that consensus will somehow break out on this deeply divisive issue. Instead the argument here has been for the need to recognize the inevitability of persisting conflict over abortion policy, and to define a way in which the appointment process might continue to operate in spite of that conflict. That is a worthy objective. The appointment process has long been an effective system for managing the strife that inevitably occurs in staffing the highest offices in the land, and the potential loss of that capability is not something we should take lightly.

The plea here is really for caution and for realism. If those who disagree about abortion are able to understand the limited opportunities the appointment process affords them for shaping abortion policy, and if they are cognizant of their ability to narrow their disagreements *within* that process, then perhaps the number of battles that will be fought on this ground can be limited to those few that hold out some hope of a meaningful victory. And if those who pursue the abortion debate in the appointment process are willing to abide by the simple and essential ground rules laid out above, then perhaps too the battles can be carried out without undermining the effectiveness of that process and without destroying the kind of civil discourse that is essential to the maintenance of legitimate forums in which a pluralist people can disagree.

John E. Jackson and Maris A. Vinovskis

Public Opinion, Elections, and the "Single-Issue" Issue

AT FIRST GLANCE, it might seem very easy to ask people whether they support or oppose legal abortions; many surveys have pursued this seemingly simple and straightforward approach. But ascertaining public opinion on controversial social issues is deceptively difficult. Conceptual and methodological problems complicate interpretation of the results. For example, differences in the way questions are worded or in the order in which they are asked can affect the findings by 10 to 15 percentage points. As a result, political leaders and the public are often baffled by the different levels of support for or opposition to legal abortion reported in the major public opinion polls. The confusion is compounded by the tendency of pro-life and pro-choice activists to quote only those statistics that seem to demonstrate that the great majority of Americans endorses their position. Even an accurate and honestly reported count of levels of public support for or opposition to legal abortion would not necessarily reveal the political significance of the issue—its importance or centrality to the electorate.

Interpreting Public Opinion

Existing data do make possible analyses of the overall distribution of positions on abortion, the individual rankings of alternative options, the relative importance of the issue to voters, and the distribution of voter preferences across electoral districts. Taken together, they lead to an interpretation of how public opinion on abortion affects elections and the electoral system; but elections and the representation system, taken over time, are the only true measures of public preferences.

Distribution of Positions

Very few individuals oppose or support abortion without reservation. The American National Election surveys for 1972, 1976, 1978, and 1980, for example, found that approximately 10 percent of adults felt that "abortion should never be permitted" while about one-quarter of them said that "abortion should never be forbidden, since one should not require a woman to have a child she doesn't want."[1] While the actual percentages vary among different surveys, the always pro-choice position is usually larger than the always pro-life one and neither extreme position attracts a majority of the population.

Most Americans favor abortion in certain situations. Their support usually distinguishes between reasons that are considered "hard" (for example, danger to mother's health) and those that are "soft" (for example, desire of married women to have no more children), with the former garnering much more support. In the American National Election studies about 90 percent of adults favored abortion "if the life and health of the woman are in danger," but less than 50 percent approved "if due to personal reasons, the woman would have difficulty in caring for the child." Thus, though most Americans favor abortion under certain restricted conditions, support falls off sharply when the rationale is the economic or personal needs of the family or the woman.

Any significant changes in public opinion on abortion over time can be detected by reviewing responses to the National Opinion Research Center (NORC) questions on abortion that have been asked repeatedly since 1965.[2] The NORC surveys asked whether it should be possible for a pregnant woman to obtain a legal abortion if the woman's health is seriously endangered by the pregnancy ("hard"), if the family has a very low income and cannot afford any more children ("soft"), or for any reason ("always").

The results of the NORC surveys confirm our earlier distinctions between "hard" and "soft" reasons in the levels of abortion support. They also reveal generally parallel changes in the levels of approval among the three options and show the sharpest increases between 1965 and 1972. A

1. The data on the American National Election surveys were made available by the Inter-University Consortium for Political and Social Research. They were originally collected by the Center for Political Studies of the Institute for Social Research, University of Michigan, under a grant from the National Science Foundation. Neither the original collectors of the data nor the consortium bear any responsibility for the analysis or interpretations presented here.

2. Helen Rose Fuchs Ebaugh and C. Allen Haney, "Shifts in Abortion Attitudes: 1972–1978," *Journal of Marriage and the Family*, vol. 42 (August 1980), pp. 491–99; Mark Evers and Jeanne McGee, "The Trend and Pattern in Attitudes Toward Abortion in the United States, 1965–1977," *Social Indicators Research*, vol. 7 (January 1980), pp. 251–67.

substantially smaller increase immediately following the Supreme Court decision on abortion in 1973 is attributable either to legitimizing effects of the Court decision or simply the continuation of the earlier liberalization trends.[3] In any case, since 1974 public support for or opposition to legal abortion has remained surprisingly constant despite an increasingly intense public struggle over the issue. Of those who had an opinion on abortion in the 1982 NORC survey, 92 percent favored abortions "if the woman's health is seriously endangered," 52 percent "if the family cannot afford any more children," and 41 percent "for any reason."[4]

Support for legal abortion depends not only on the specific reasons for having one, but also on when it is performed. Americans are more likely to support abortion, for whatever reason, in the first trimester of pregnancy than in the second or third trimesters. Thus, support for abortion if the woman's life is endangered drops 12 percentage points when the question distinguishes between first and second trimester abortions.[5] This suggests that those who wish to curtail rather than entirely eliminate abortions might be able to maximize public support for their position by differentiating between first and second trimester abortions. No political leader or group has yet espoused such an approach.

Individual Rankings of Alternative Options

So far we have suggested that public opinion is fairly evenly divided on the abortion issue with only a minority favoring either an absolute ban on all abortions or allowing them for any reason. A majority favors abortion under some conditions—especially when the pregnancy endangers the life of the mother or is likely to result in a seriously deformed child. But what happens to the majority if the conditions change? Are its moderate members more likely to support the pro-life or pro-choice position? The subsequent behavior of this middle group is particularly important since the political agenda, as set forth by activists on both sides, tends toward the

3. Donald Granberg and Beth Wellman Granberg, "Abortion Attitudes, 1965–1980: Trends and Determinants," *Family Planning Perspectives*, vol. 12 (September–October 1980), pp. 250–61; Judith Blake, "The Abortion Decisions: Judicial Review and Public Opinion," in Edward Manier, William Liu, and David Soloman, eds., *Abortion: New Directions for Policy Studies* (University of Notre Dame Press, 1977), pp. 51–82.

4. Thomas W. Smith, National Opinion Research Center, telephone interview.

5. *The Gallup Opinion Index*, Report 153, April 1978; *The Gallup Opinion Index*, Report 166, May 1979.

extremes rather than any of the middle positions favored by a popular majority.

Many surveys show consistent pro-choice supporters usually to outnumber consistent pro-life respondents by at least as much as 2 to 1. Consequently, one might speculate that when individuals in the middle are forced to choose sides, enough of them would gravitate toward the consistent pro-choice position to provide it a comfortable majority. This would be especially true if a substantial proportion of those who support legal abortion for either "hard" or "soft" reasons are simply unwilling to accept a total ban on all abortions.

None of the surveys on abortion asks respondents what alternative option they would favor if the one they selected was unavailable to them. Blake and Del Pinal, however, have tried to estimate how persons in the middle might respond by comparing their background characteristics and attitudes on other issues with those of extreme pro-life and extreme pro-choice supporters. Those in the middle, Blake and Del Pinal conclude, are much closer in both personal characteristics and attitudes to the pro-life than to the pro-choice position. They argue that people who equivocate on abortion should be seen as "closet negatives," who account for the recent political successes of the pro-life movement despite an apparent overwhelming majority in favor of legal abortion, at least under some restricted conditions.[6]

An indication of how people in the middle may react if their initial preferences become unattainable is provided by responses to abortion questions that provide options only at the extremes. When individuals are asked if they support or oppose the Supreme Court's legalization of abortion, or if they support or oppose the human life bill, many are being asked to agree or disagree with a position that is considerably more extreme than their preferred stance. In most of these situations, a majority continues either to support legalized abortion or to oppose any proposed outright ban, but the split is often quite close.[7] Thus, Blake and Del Pinal probably are correct in seeing many of those in the middle as "closet negatives," but they may have exaggerated the extent of this phenomenon in view of the persistence of a pro-choice majority.

6. Judith Blake and Jorge H. Del Pinal, "Negativism, Equivocation, and Wobbly Assent: Public 'Support' for the Prochoice Platform on Abortion," *Demography*, vol. 18 (August 1981), pp. 309–20.

7. Granberg and Granberg, "Abortion Attitudes"; Ebaugh and Haney, "Shifts in Abortion Attitudes"; Frederick S. Jaffe, Barbara L. Lindheim, and Philip R. Lee, *Abortion Politics: Private Morality and Public Policy* (McGraw-Hill, 1981), pp. 99–111.

Relative Importance of the Issue

Even if the distribution of initial and subsequent preferences on abortion was known, additional information would be needed to assess the impact of the issue on elections. How important is abortion compared to other issues for that individual (centrality)? How strongly does someone feel about the abortion issue (intensity)? And finally, how willing is the individual to act upon her or his convictions because of abortion (behavior)?

Many observers see the abortion issue as particularly important to voters. For example, Anthony Lewis of the *New York Times* has written:

> Over the last few years political analysts have noted the significance of the single-issue voter: the person who cares only about a candidate's views on gun control, for example, or busing, or capital punishment. It is clear now, I think, that one such issue is likely to have the largest impact on American politics for the longest time. That is abortion.[8]

Despite the widespread notion that abortion is one of today's most important political issues, survey evidence suggests just the opposite—few individuals rank the abortion issue as one of their top priorities. When Roper pollsters asked voters in 1976 to rank fifteen policy issues in order of importance, a constitutional amendment prohibiting abortions was chosen by only 4 percent of the respondents and ranked last.[9] Similarly, in 1976 when voters were given a list of twenty-five issues, they ranked abortion in last place.[10] In the American National Election study for 1978, respondents were asked what they thought were the most important problems facing this country. While nearly 65 percent said inflation was a major national problem, fewer than 0.5 percent mentioned abortion—a finding that matches previous results from that same survey in 1972, 1974, and 1976.[11] Finally, when Gallup polled individuals in January 1982 on the most important problem facing this country today, 49 percent said the high cost of living or inflation, 28 percent mentioned unemployment or the recession, and only 4 percent volunteered the moral decline in the country.[12] In other words, most Americans tend to be much more concerned about economic issues than social and moral ones such as abortion. Only a small minority of the public sees abortion as one of its most important concerns.

If most Americans do not regard abortion as one of the most important

8. Anthony Lewis, "A Singular Issue," *The New York Times* (November 16, 1981).

9. Cited in Jaffe, Lindheim, and Lee, *Abortion Politics*, p. 107.

10. "Counting the Catholics," *Newsweek*, September 20, 1976.

11. Michael W. Traugott and Maris A. Vinovskis, "Abortion and the 1978 Congressional Elections," *Family Planning Perspectives*, vol. 12 (September–October 1980), pp. 238–46.

12. *The Gallup Opinion Index*, Report 198, March 1982.

issues, do those who do regard it as very important differ significantly from the rest of the population in their attitude about legal abortion? If the small minority that feels intensely about this issue and calls it a central concern is heavily weighted toward either the pro-life or pro-choice perspective, this factor could have a bearing on how the issue affects electoral politics.

Again, very few systematic efforts have been made to ascertain the general public's intensity of feeling on the abortion issue. A recent analysis by Schuman and Presser, however, provides some leads.[13] Though their national samples are small, the results are quite striking. After inquiring whether "a woman should be allowed to have an abortion in the early months of pregnancy if she wants one," they asked two additional questions to elicit respondents' intensity of feeling on the issue as well as its centrality for them. Schuman and Presser found that individuals who felt strongly about abortion compared to other public issues were much more likely to oppose early abortion than to favor it. Similarly, those who said that a candidate's position on abortion is very important when they decide how to vote in a congressional election were much more opposed to abortion than those who did not consider it an important issue. The limited sample size precludes any definitive statements based on this study, but it does suggest that among those most emotionally involved and concerned about abortion, the pro-life position is heavily overrepresented.

Several other studies have found that pro-life supporters seem more single-minded and determined than their pro-choice counterparts. But the studies do not show how this affects actual behavior and actual outcomes. Henshaw and Martire, for example, have found that a higher percentage of those opposing legal abortion than those favoring it say they are more likely to vote solely on the basis of candidates' positions on abortion (41 percent versus 35 percent). The net effect, however, actually supports pro-choice candidates (23 percent versus 12 percent) because of the larger number of pro-choice supporters in the population.[14] On the other hand, in analyzing the reported behavior of both sides, Schuman and Presser found that among those endorsing the pro-life position, 8.3 percent had written a letter and 5.6 percent had contributed money, while among those supporting the pro-choice option, 1.5 percent had written a letter and 4.1 percent had

13. Howard Schuman and Stanley Presser, *Questions and Answers in Attitude Surveys: Experiments on Question Form, Wording, and Context* (Academic Press, 1981).

14. Stanley K. Henshaw and Greg Martire, "Abortion and Public Opinion Polls," *Family Planning Perspectives*, vol. 14 (March–April 1982), pp. 53–60.

given money.[15] Similarly, a Gallup Poll in June 1981 found that 4 percent of Americans belonged to or contributed to organizations that oppose abortion while only 1 percent belonged to or contributed to organizations that support legal abortions.[16]

There is no reliable estimate of the percentage of the electorate that can be tagged as single-issue voters on the basis of their stance on abortion. Once people are inside the voting booth, they must consider all of the alternatives available to them. Simply asking whether someone would vote for or against a candidate on the basis of his or her position on abortion probably exaggerates greatly the strength of this issue. On the other hand, estimates of those who have written letters, contributed money, or joined an organization on behalf of the abortion issue may underestimate its importance. Many people probably feel quite strongly about abortion policy, but do not trouble themselves to write, contribute, or join. One suspects that as the issue continues to attract attention, especially if a constitutional amendment prohibiting abortions becomes a real possibility, the number of activists on both sides will increase considerably. When the June 1981 Gallup poll on membership and contributions to special interest groups asked individuals if they would like to join one of the groups concerned with the abortion issue, another 5 percent said they would like to join a pro-life organization and 3 percent more would join a pro-choice group. There is considerable room for expansion of membership and contributions for both sides. But pro-life forces are likely to command more than a 2 to 1 margin over their opponents if both sides are able to mobilize potential supporters.

Distribution of Preferences among Districts

Understanding the distribution across electoral districts of supporters and opponents of legal abortion is important to an assessment of its impact on elections. Though only a small minority of the general public feels very strongly about the abortion issue, if it were concentrated in certain areas, it could exercise much more influence on elections in those areas than on elections in the country as a whole. Further, if the distribution were such that strong proponents on both sides of this issue were separated from each other regionally, the controversy over abortion could become a sectional battle, as was the antebellum struggle over slavery.

Since there is no direct information about voter preferences on the abor-

15. Schuman and Presser, *Questions and Answers in Attitude Surveys.*
16. *The Gallup Opinion Index*, Report 191, August 1981.

tion issue according to electoral districts, we can only estimate that distribution from the socioeconomic and geographic characteristics of supporters and opponents. If the pro-life and pro-choice sides are highly differentiated in terms of their background characteristics, one might expect a higher concentration of each of them in areas with a disproportionate number of individuals with those special characteristics. If the sides are relatively similar to each other in terms of personal characteristics, it is much more likely that they will be more or less evenly distributed across electoral districts.

Almost all of the studies of public opinion on abortion have found surprisingly small differences in the socioeconomic and geographic characteristics of the populations on each side. Generally, the higher the socioeconomic status of the individual, the more likely he or she is to approve of legal abortion (with formal education being the best predictor). There are few sex differences in attitudes on abortion. Age is slightly inversely correlated with approval of abortion. Blacks are more likely than whites to oppose abortion, a difference largely explained by blacks' greater religiosity. Rural areas tend to be more pro-life than urban or suburban ones. There are significant regional variations: the highest level of approval for abortion occurs in the Pacific, New England, and mid-Atlantic states while the lowest support is in the south central states. Though there are important socioeconomic and geographic differences in abortion attitudes, they are not very large statistically and usually account for only 8 to 10 percent of the variance.[17]

The religious background of respondents helps to explain variations in abortion attitudes. Support for legal abortion is highest among Jews and lowest among Catholics. However, only 1 percent of the variation in opinions about abortion reflected over time in the NORC surveys is attributable to Protestant-Catholic differences. Indeed, variations within the five major Protestant groups are larger than those between Catholics and Protestants in the aggregate. Among Protestants, Episcopalians are the most supportive of legal abortion and Baptists the most opposed. There is a statistically significant relationship between religiosity and abortion attitudes. For example, the more frequently someone attends religious services, the more likely he or she is to oppose abortion.[18] As a result, districts with larger

17. Ebaugh and Haney, "Shifts in Abortion Attitudes"; Evers and McGee, "Trend and Pattern in Attitudes Toward Abortion"; Granberg and Granberg, "Abortion Attitudes"; Blake and Del Pinal, "Negativism, Equivocation, and Wobbly Assent."
18. Granberg and Granberg, "Abortion Attitudes."

concentrations of religiously active individuals will probably have a stronger pro-life orientation than the country as a whole. Nevertheless, even taking religion into consideration, attitudes about legalization of abortion probably do not vary markedly by electoral district.

Elections and the Politics of Abortion

In the 1960s and early 1970s, efforts to repeal restrictive abortion laws often focused on elections as a way of influencing legislators or of bypassing them entirely with referenda. Many of the campaigns for abortion reform, especially such early efforts as those in Colorado and North Carolina, for example, were relatively low key. The emphasis was on educating the public and drawing support from influential members of the legislature. In these cases, the election of members usually did not play an important role, and abortion did not become a key election issue. Since the emphasis was on developing a reform package that was politically acceptable to a broad spectrum of legislators, the bills passed were patterned after the American Law Institute Model Abortion Law, which left abortion to the discretion of physicians rather than of women themselves.

As the proponents of more extreme abortion reform gained ascendancy and called for the abolition of any abortion restrictions and the pro-life forces organized in opposition, the state battles became more intense and more likely to involve the targeting of opposition legislators. In New York State, for example, the fight over abortion raged not only in the halls of the legislature but also in the election districts. The pro-life and pro-choice forces mounted extensive local campaigns to punish and reward individual legislators on the basis of their positions on abortion.

Finding that organized pro-life opposition to repeal of restrictive abortion statutes was becoming increasingly effective in many states, the pro-choice movement in the state of Washington switched to another electoral mechanism—the popular referendum. In a bitterly contested referendum, the voters in Washington State approved the legalization of abortion by a vote of 56 to 44 percent. This was the first time that the abortion issue had been placed directly before the electorate. The success of the referendum approach in Washington State as well as some legislative setbacks elsewhere encouraged pro-choice activists to try to replicate the Washington experience elsewhere. Legalization of abortion was placed on the ballot in North Dakota and Michigan in 1972, but was defeated in both states.

Whatever trend toward easing restrictions on abortion had developed in the states during the late 1960s and early 1970s thus encountered setbacks at the polls on the eve of the Supreme Court decision in *Roe* v. *Wade.*

That decision shifted the focus from the states to Washington, D.C., and had a dual effect on the electoral politics of abortion. Although the pro-choice movement had not always persuaded the electorate or state legislatures to repeal the remaining restrictions on abortion, now the Supreme Court simply declared such restrictions unconstitutional. One effect was to render existing state-level pro-choice organizations nonessential since the Court had achieved their goals for them. A second effect was to outrage pro-life forces because the Court allowed women more ready access to abortion than did most of the state reform statutes and even more ready access than the general public supported, according to polls. At the same time, by giving abortion constitutional protection, the Court made irrelevant ordinary legislative actions at either state or federal level and state referenda results. With pro-life forces shocked by the Court decision and split on the exact wording of a proposal for a constitutional amendment, state-level pro-choice groups disbanded, victory seemingly achieved. The National Abortion Rights Action League (NARAL) established itself in Washington as a national-level lobby group to handle any pro-choice needs that might arise.

Neither the pro-life nor the pro-choice forces prepared effectively for the 1974 congressional elections. Little early effort was made to develop an effective grass-roots organization that could be mobilized at elections on behalf of pro-choice candidates. Although several congressmen were targeted by pro-life groups in 1974, a survey of House and Senate contests for that year revealed that abortion was not a major campaign issue.[19]

From an electoral perspective, 1976 was a watershed year for the abortion issue. The pro-life forces, slow to develop an extensive local network across the country, received an important boost on November 25, 1975, when the National Council of Catholic Bishops, in a highly unusual move, adopted a "Pastoral Plan for Pro-Life Activities." The Pastoral Plan called upon all Catholic-sponsored or Catholic-related agencies to support "a comprehensive pro-life legislative" program that included the passage of a constitutional amendment to protect the life of the unborn child. Not only did the Pastoral Plan set forth a legislative package, it also urged the faithful to organize locally in order to elect sympathetic congressmen in

19. Jeannie Rosoff, "Is Support of Abortion Political Suicide?" *Family Planning Perspectives*, vol. 7 (January–February 1975), pp. 13–22.

1976. Though the plan did not result in an extensive network of pro-life organizations in each congressional district, it did provide an impetus for further efforts at the local level and legitimized and spurred the campaign activities of individuals. The National Council of Bishops continued its political involvement in 1976 with an expression of disappointment in Jimmy Carter's abortion views after a meeting with him. While the council focused on organizing potential voters in each district and commenting on the position of the presidential candidates on abortion, Ellen McCormack ran as a pro-life candidate in the Democratic presidential primaries and raised enough money in twenty states to qualify for matching federal funds. If her campaign failed to generate much excitement or attract many voters, it helped to publicize the pro-life position in a series of early primary states.

Also in 1976 the first Hyde amendment was passed, restricting the use of federal funds to pay for abortions. This demonstrated to the pro-life movement that there were significant legislative gains to be made in Congress even while a human life amendment remained bottled up in committee. The Hyde amendment also reminded those in the pro-choice camp that the battle for abortion on demand was far from over. Thus the National Abortion Rights Action League and the National Right to Life Committee (NRLC) were spurred to greater political activity both internally and externally as the publicity about the Hyde amendment stimulated additional contributions and added members to both sides.

From an electoral perspective, the Hyde amendment had another important effect. For each side, the outcomes of congressional elections were now judged by estimates of votes to be lost or gained for the Hyde amendment in the ensuing Congress. In fact, the struggle over the exact wording of the Hyde amendment from year to year became a highly symbolic issue —especially since the net effect of changes in the wording of that amendment had very little impact on the number of federally funded abortions. Yet enactment of a slightly more restrictive Hyde amendment became either a major achievement or a severe disappointment to the respective sides and stimulated each of them to even greater efforts in the next congressional elections.

Passage of the Hyde amendment also helped to revitalize local pro-life and pro-choice activities that had languished after the Supreme Court decisions had shifted the focus to Washington. Since states could continue to fund abortions if they so desired, enactment of the Hyde amendment seemed an empty gesture unless it was accompanied by comparable restrictions in the states. As a result, state battles over abortion policy regained some of the vitality lost after the Supreme Court decisions and in the process reinforced efforts to build strong local organizations.

Abortion was never an important factor in the 1976 presidential campaign, a conclusion substantiated by a statistical analysis of the American National Election postelection survey of voters.[20] Pro-life activists failed to make abortion one of the key issues in the election, but they did succeed in pushing reluctant presidential candidates to take a position on abortion—usually to some extent critical of the Supreme Court decision. Pro-life groups did seem more effective in mobilizing and publicizing their efforts in this election than did their pro-choice counterparts. In any case, the presidential election of 1976 and the passage of the Hyde amendment that same year stimulated both the NRLC and NARAL to focus even more attention on elections in the future. Whereas electoral politics played a relatively minor role in the thinking and activity of both sides in the first few years following the Supreme Court decision of 1973, electoral politics occupied center stage after 1976 as both pro-life and pro-choice activists determined to prove their effectiveness in the 1978 congressional elections. That intensified commitment to electoral politics was reflected, in part, in the creation of the National Abortion Rights Action League Political Action Committee (NARAL-PAC) and its pro-life counterpart, the Life Amendment Political Action Committee (LAPAC).

While many commentators on the 1978 congressional elections have argued that abortion was a key factor in those elections, the work of Traugott and Vinovskis casts doubt on that interpretation. The amount of money raised and contributed to candidates by each abortion-related political action committee was insignificant compared to contributions from other such committees. Even in the particular races that LAPAC or NARAL-PAC supported, money contributed by either group represented only a very small portion of the total money spent by the candidates. Interviews before and after the election with the campaign managers in eighty-six contested House districts failed to turn up any evidence that abortion was an important factor in those races. A survey of public opinion in those House districts found that only a minority of the respondents identified any one issue as important in that contest, and less than 1 percent mentioned abortion as a key factor.[21] Finally, even in the highly publicized defeat of

20. Maris A. Vinovskis, "Abortion and the Presidential Election of 1976: A Multivariate Analysis of Voting Behavior," in Carl E. Schneider and Maris A. Vinovskis, eds., *The Law and Politics of Abortion* (Lexington Books, 1980), pp. 184–205.

21. Traugott and Vinovskis, "Abortion and the 1978 Congressional Elections."

pro-choice Senator Dick Clark, preliminary analysis of data from a post-election survey shows no evidence that the abortion issue had any more to do with his loss than other problems he had with his constituents.[22] Both pro-life and pro-choice forces plunged into the 1978 congressional elections with unprecedented zeal and determination, but they probably had relatively little impact on voters' decisions to support or oppose any particular candidate.

Although the abortion issue was not a major determinant of voting behavior in 1978, the results of those congressional elections did have a major impact on both sides. The pro-life forces benefited greatly from the news media portrayal of the elections as a pro-life victory—an interpretation reinforced by Senator Clark's postelection announcement that it was the abortion issue that had defeated him. In addition, the pro-life position in Congress was substantially enhanced by the addition of new members who happened to be more likely to vote against federal funding of abortions than their predecessors. In the House of Representatives, for example, few incumbents were defeated for any reason, but in districts with open seats the newly elected members tended to be more pro-life—not because of any direct pressure from their constituents in the election, but because of their personal conservatism on social issues. Pro-life forces made significant inroads in Congress by reinforcing the idea among politicians that their organizations were important in congressional elections and by the election of generally more conservative members.

For all of the apparent benefit to the pro-life side, in 1980 the abortion issue once again does not appear to have been an important influence on the electoral results. It was not frequently mentioned by voters, for example, as one of the most important issues facing the country. Though the differentiation on the presidential candidates' position on abortion was much sharper than in 1976, an analysis of the determinants of voting for the presidency found that a voter's position on abortion was not a good predictor of whether the vote was cast for Anderson, Carter, or Reagan.[23]

Nevertheless, the 1980 election became a stunning success for the pro-life movement with the victory of Ronald Reagan and the defeat of liberal senators like Birch Bayh, John Culver, George McGovern, Jacob Javits, and Frank Church. With those defeats and the new Republican majority, the Senate, which had been a pro-choice stronghold, became both more

22. Vinovskis, preliminary multiple classification analysis of individual-level data.
23. Vinovskis, preliminary multiple classification analysis of the 1980 presidential election using the American National Election survey data.

conservative and more pro-life. A constitutional amendment that had seemed a remote possibility now seems much less so. Reagan's election and the appointment of a few pro-life activists to key positions in the federal bureaucracy may mean that the movement will be able to influence administrative decisions related to abortions. Furthermore, while more extreme elements have often dominated many of the pro-life organizations and set their agenda, the appointment of some more moderate pro-life leaders to administrative positions may reinforce or even reestablish their credibility within the pro-life movement.

The 1978 and 1980 elections brought about a growth of pro-life support in the Congress although abortion by no means dominated or controlled those elections. One manifestation of that growth is the virtually uncontested acceptance of restrictions on federal funding of abortions. Looking ahead, NARAL has all but acknowledged the increased pro-life strength by fundamentally revising its political strategy to emphasize more effort at the local level in order to block state-level ratification of any potential constitutional amendment. Thus, though races for federal offices can be expected to be bitterly contested by both sides in the future, there will probably be more political involvement in state legislative races as well. The benefits to the pro-life side stemming from the outcomes of the elections of 1978 and 1980 presage increasing attention on the constitutional amendment process.

Single-Issue Politics and American Governance

The abortion issue is an excellent test case of the implications of intense, single-issue politics for the American governmental system. Current policy was set dramatically and abruptly by the Supreme Court and differs substantially from previous policies. Opinion data indicate there is a fairly wide distribution of preferences, and that persons with pro-life preferences are much more likely to attach great importance to this issue than to others, thus fitting the definition of single-issue politics. Interest groups on each side are organized to fulfill a single purpose and have little incentive to engage in compromise, negotiation, or coalition building that might divert them from their purpose or weaken them organizationally. These circumstances, plus recent political activity of pro-life groups and a few well-publicized defeats of pro-choice legislators, would seem to epitomize the single-issue threat.

We see little threat to the political system from the continued interest in single-issue politics. The natural characteristics of the American political process, including its reliance on single-member districts and plurality winners, the multi-issue character of the society and its politics, and the natural weakening of single-issue interest groups as they begin to succeed all make it unlikely that conflict over a single issue will distort the character of the electoral system. That judgment is supported by the empirical evidence relating to public opinion on the abortion issue and the evidence relating to the evolution of policy outcomes and interest group behavior.

No matter how extreme and intense the character of participants and groups in the abortion controversy, the distribution of public opinion across states and congressional districts militates against a divisive regional or sectional clash such as occurred over slavery. People with various preferences about abortion policy are found in virtually all districts and certainly in all states. There is no primary concentration in particular states and regions; small geographic concentrations are overshadowed by very viable pro-choice and pro-life groups operating in most if not all states. Elections, because they are the focus of attention, may be strongly contested, but the distribution of preferences should be less polarized in Congress than in society as a whole.

Nor are pressures arising from the abortion issue likely to produce electoral conflict of an extreme character. In spite of the claims made by some interest groups and political action committees, the evidence does not support the claim that positions on the abortion issue were critical in defeating very many, if any, candidates in 1978 and 1980. It is easy for pressure groups, and very much in their organizational interests, to target vulnerable incumbents, to generate extensive publicity about campaign efforts, and then to claim a decisive role in the victory of the challenger. Losers in these contests have an incentive to overstate the importance of being targeted as an explanation for their defeat. Once these claims are subjected to empirical analysis and the relative importance of the abortion issue determined, there will likely be a diminution both of influence of these interest groups and of concern about their ability to dominate electoral politics.

The most important factor in diminishing the importance of single-issue political groups is that most policymaking in this country is done by legislators and executives chosen in single-winner, plurality-determined elections. For any particular policy interests to become effective in such a system, they must eventually form coalitions with other interests in support of specific candidates and political organizations. This process can occur implicitly and without formal agreements as different organizations decide which candidates to support and promote. Even if this electoral activity begins with a single-issue candidate, appeals and accommodations must be broadened to build a sufficient electoral base to obtain a plurality. The ability of a single-issue interest group to withstand these pressures will depend upon the nature and importance of other issues at the time and upon the availability and role of money, publicity, and volunteers in the electoral process.

The more the electoral process is dominated by many small, diffuse issues and the more the special interest groups control the resources, the longer the single-issue groups can maintain their singular identity and influence. Eventually, however, these interest groups must join or forge broader issue clusters and back candidates and parties with more general appeals.

This process of absorption into broader, less extreme coalitions and eventually into one of the major political parties describes the history of single-issue politics in this country and is the current direction of the various sides in the abortion conflict. Pro-choice groups are increasingly aligned with other groups promoting parts of the liberal agenda, especially those aimed at benefiting women and the poor. The coalition includes a variety of professional social service organizations and currently an alliance with the Democratic party. On the other side, pro-life organizations are associated increasingly with an array of diverse religious and socially conservative organizations trying to change federal policy on school prayer, busing, and the social spending issues identified with the liberal constituencies.

Recent Republican party efforts to develop a Republican majority mean that the social-issues coalition may be swept into a broad political entity that includes interests in economic and foreign policy issues, many of which historically have been quite different from and even antithetical to those of the antiabortion constituency. For example, economic conservatives who traditionally have been upper-class Protestants opposed to an interventionist federal government have not been associated with the core pro-life groups, which are more closely linked to Catholic and fundamentalist Protestant churches. This process of political assimilation will weaken the extreme single-issue groups on both sides. The dilemma they face is to participate in these broader groups in order to achieve some of their policy objectives or to maintain their organizational identity and strength at the cost of a smaller impact.

Absorption into the party coalitions would mean that future electoral successes of pro-life and pro-choice groups would depend on successes of the respective political parties. The latter, in turn, depend on party positions and policies on a range of issues. If the Reagan administration, and specifically the conservative political movement, founders on any of the economic, social, or foreign policy positions it has taken, the influence of the pro-life organizations will be diminished regardless of public preferences on the abortion issue. Similarly, pro-choice interests lost strength by virtue of their identification with the liberal agenda and with the Carter administration, which was generally rejected by the voters in 1980—although the 1980 election said nothing about voter preferences on abortion.

Identification with a successful political coalition carries costs as well as benefits for single-issue groups. As public policy is deemed more responsive to one or the other set of interests, the ability of the apparent winner to mobilize members and stimulate activity is diminished. Pro-choice interests felt this loss following the *Roe* v. *Wade* decision. We contend that pro-life groups have not been able to impart their previous sense of urgency since adoption of the Hyde amendment and inclusion of pro-life partisans in the Reagan administration. The combined effect of the latter two events is to move abortion policy in the pro-life direction, thus weakening the relative ability of pro-life interest groups to mobilize volunteers and obtain contributions. These policy changes have also provided the basis for more activity on the part of the pro-choice groups. Paradoxical as it may appear, partial victories seem to strengthen the losers while simultaneously weakening the winners.

Finally, the potential role of abortion as a disruptive single issue will be moderated if conflict shifts increasingly from the national to the state level. That shift would occur if Congress should propose a pro-life constitutional amendment for ratification by the states, or if a trend toward enhanced state discretionary authority is sustained. In the case of a constitutional amendment, the pro-choice side would likely follow the strategy used by the groups opposed to the equal rights amendment and organize at the state level in enough states to try to frustrate ratification. The strong bias for the status quo in the ratification process allows a single legislative chamber in as few as thirteen states to bar ratification. That factor would advantage the pro-choice side, as it advantaged opponents of the ERA. In any event, the need for both sides to concentrate activity at the state level would diminish the volume and intensity of conflict at the national level, both within Congress and in Senate and House elections. Similarly, enhanced state discretionary authority, stemming either from favorable judicial decisions or congressional action, would weaken the size, influence, and resources of the various national interest groups. They might remain active in individual states, and certainly would try to recruit members and raise money on a national basis. However, with the emphasis on state politics, they would not have the strong unifying target needed to mobilize large numbers of people or raise large amounts of money as they have in the recent past.

In sum, we do not see any peril to the traditional electoral process from active, well-organized, single-issue political groups that focus on either pro-choice or pro-life policy. Our analyses of the nature of electoral politics and interest groups, America's experience with various social policy interest groups, the distribution of preferences among electoral districts, and our observation of recent abortion politics all indicate that the electoral system is in little danger of being damaged by the abortion policy controversy.

Gilbert Y. Steiner

Reactions of the Symposium

THE Brookings symposium on the abortion dispute and the American system engaged political activists and scholars in an examination of the effects of the abortion dispute on governmental institutions and the norms of political conduct. This meeting of pro-life and pro-choice forces and specialists in American government from a variety of disciplines—political science, history, journalism, law—was not an everyday event. Activists on the respective sides normally meet only at congressional hearings where each group speaks separately to the merits of its cause. The symposium was not a forum for the presentation of substantive views or a collective bargaining session to achieve agreement between antagonists. Rather it was a way of collectively evaluating any unanticipated consequences that the struggle over abortion policy may have had for the American system.

In order that there might be a common starting point for discussion, the research essays that constitute the preceding chapters were distributed to symposium participants well in advance. Roughly coincident with the period between distribution of the essays and the meeting of the symposium on September 24, 1982, the U.S. Senate engaged in prolonged if not constant debate on a proposal to bar direct or indirect federal financial support of abortion and to facilitate Supreme Court review of state and local antiabortion measures. Participants in the symposium obviously brought with them their individual evaluations of that Senate debate, which ended with a successful motion to table the restrictive proposal after three cloture motions to break an opposition filibuster all failed.

The format of the symposium allowed each writer to present the highlights of his work, but in the main the participants themselves controlled the direction of the discussion. The result was a review of most of the judgments that together point to what I characterized in the introduction to this volume as a sanguine view about the governmental and political consequences of the abortion dispute. Although the discussion focused on governmental institutions, abortion policy was its point of departure, so differences of opinion were understandably sharp. The underlying conflict over policy was repressed, but could not be suppressed, and some academic participants came to appreciate the value of rules for debate on abortion. Nonetheless, every effort was made to permit all participants to speak to the issues raised. No votes were taken. The following account of the discussions, however, reveals a widespread disposition—but not a universal one—to agree that unwise as some may consider the results, the fight over abortion policy has not yet at least proved destructive or intolerably costly to governmental institutions.

Constitutional Legitimacy

In response to Lawrence Friedman's assertions that in the long view of constitutional interpretation there is neither "something illegitimate" about the *Roe* v. *Wade* decision nor about overturning it, participants expressed their discomfort by nibbling around the edges of Friedman's proposition rather than making broadside attacks on it. Friedman was asked if he believed any Supreme Court opinion could be "illegitimate." Not all participants were comfortable with his response that while there may be unwise decisions, it is hard to envisage an illegitimate Supreme Court decision. His explanation was that controversial decisions that ultimately become embodied in the social and political system cease to be thought of as illegitimate. *Brown* v. *Board of Education*, striking down the separate but equal doctrine, is a case in point. Constitutional scholars were once troubled by that decision, but it soon became unquestionable. If, on the other hand, the Court misjudges popular temper, constitutional scholars shy away from accepting the decision. In this respect, Friedman argued, constitutional scholarship may be somewhat parasitic. It is too early, however, to know whether *Roe* is acquiring greater legitimacy in the manner of *Brown*.

Others emphasized that *Roe* v. *Wade* leaves people on all sides uncomfortable. It represents a striking deviation from the norm in several particulars. One is the Court's implicit dependence on substantive due process although it had, in the earlier *Griswold* case, been reluctant to admit such dependence. The *Roe* decision, furthermore, is unique among constitutional cases in its base in the state of medical science. Again, *Roe* is a judicial finding that is said to "look" more like a legislative enactment than a court opinion because of the detailed specification of changing state authority at various stages of a pregnancy. And even the Court itself seems somewhat uncomfortable, it was said, or else it would not have backed away from *Roe* in the *Harris* v. *McRae* decision, upholding the ban on medicaid financing and in effect sustaining the denial of what it had termed a constitutional right.

If, to some participants, these peculiarities represent excessive judicial activism, to Friedman and others they reflect only a sensible way of dealing with a hard problem. Does it really matter, this latter group asked, to other than a handful of legal scholars whether the Court hooks its finding to substantive due process, with which it is sometimes uncomfortable, or to equal protection? And the manner in which the majority opinion in *Roe* details by trimester the limits of state authority to regulate abortion was defended as a way by which the Court foreclosed "interminable wrangling" that might have resulted from the enunciation of a principle without implementing guidelines. But many participants could not accept this rationalization for the judicial activism that they see in *Roe,* an activism that they view as a distortion of the American system.

In any event, the Supreme Court obviously erred if it expected that its clear-cut and detailed rule would put an end to controversy. The Court, after all, has no way of accurately foretelling the reaction to its decisions. When it was later confronted with the funding issue, the Court, in the view of some participants, simply recognized that wide public support had been enlisted for the restriction involved and accepted it. Other participants offered a different interpretation—that the question posed by the case was whether Congress or the Court controls the public purse, and that on that issue the Court had to back off or suffer retribution. Whatever the reason, however, the outcome reflected restraint—a willingness of the Court to bend on an aspect of abortion rights that it realized to be a weak point.

Some academic participants observed that both the federal system and the separation of powers doctrine might have been better served if the Court had declined to rule on abortion. While pro-choice people denied that the Court damaged itself by the decision, they acknowledged that the *Roe* decision came before a national consensus had evolved on the shape of abortion policy, and that the timing of the decision was probably not helpful politically. From the pro-life side, it was argued that the Court might have denied review, that it chose to decide where it need not have decided. But this kind of restraint, the answer came back, would not serve the American system well. If the Court denied review consistently, the issue would be decided circuit by circuit on a nonnational basis, an unsatisfactory way to deal with a claimed constitutional right. In response to the pro-life claim that *Roe* created a constitutional right to abortion out of whole cloth, supporters of *Roe* held that a strict textual reading of constitutional rights would mean the Court could vindicate virtually none of the rights presently deemed important.

No support seemed evident for the idea that the Constitution should be a lean document unencumbered by references to abortion. Some discussion was stimulated by the musings of an activist from the pro-choice side, which presently has little or nothing to gain from formal constitutional change, about the value of a "positive" amendment that would affirm a right to choose abortion. Others observed that while one effect of an affirming amendment would be to certify the validity of *Roe* v. *Wade*, another would be to confer doubtful status on other controversial decisions not subsequently affirmed by constitutional amendment. In the course of discussion about an amendment to affirm or one to overturn, the argument that the written Constitution is an unsuitable repository for an abortion amendment was advanced only obliquely via a reference to "inappropriate statutory responses" in the Constitution.

In sum, Friedman's joint theses—that *Roe* v. *Wade* is not out of line in that it builds reasonably on a preexisting foundation, but that overturning *Roe* v. *Wade* by law or amendment would not be out of line either—did not evoke unreserved acceptance. Some kind of formal constitutional amendment on the subject would clearly sit easier with some scholars and activists. Neither that preference nor one for a less "legislation-like" opinion led participants to view the disagreements over *Roe* v. *Wade* as posing a threat to the constitutional system.

Congress

Deliberations in Congress on abortion policy may have been inconclusive and unsatisfactory, according to Roger Davidson, but the tactics that have been employed are well within the bounds of the usual practices and so-called rules of the game. The results need not be wise or compassionate. And the processes that produce them need not have been neat and orderly, but only regarded as within Congress's usual ways of doing its business.

Davidson acknowledged to symposium participants that by ideal standards of procedure and decisionmaking, Congress can be faulted on numerous aspects of its consideration of the abortion issue: committee hearings have been few and far between; markup sessions have been challenged as unfair; floor debate, at least until the 1982 filibuster, has been surprisingly brief, and even in the course of the filibuster, the debate strayed from the issue. Pro-choice forces have pushed their cause by attempting to discourage hearings and to keep restrictive legislation bottled up in committee, while pro-life forces have pushed theirs with the appropriations rider and with floor amendments that short-circuit committee action.

Congressional scholars among the participants emphasized that Congress should not be expected to achieve a conclusive resolution of the abortion dispute. Congress is simply not a consensus-forming entity. Often for political reasons, it is organized to avoid dealing with sharply controversial issues, to wait instead for a popular consensus to form. Congressional strength does not lie in the clarification of difficult issues. Moreover, the important changes associated with the "democratization" of Congress in recent years further hamper its ability to effect policy compromises. Davidson's picture of an inconclusive, even messy, kind of response by Congress to the abortion dispute should thus be seen as one characteristic of the institution.

Some pro-choice persons are disposed to push the argument an additional step. They agree that Congress is incapable of resolving the abortion dispute but find the explanation as much in the issue as in the institution. Beyond the limitations that make it hard for Congress to deal with most controversial questions is the fact that a great majority of the members would rather not deal with abortion because the polarizing nature of the issue jeopardizes reelection. In this view, abortion policymaking is especially suited to the judicial branch, where the putative political risks of making abortion policy can be absorbed.

Most participants acknowledged that many of the legislative tactics used in the abortion controversy are not unique to it, but some expressed reservations about excessive deference legislators have shown some of their colleagues who hold extreme positions. The importance of the issue and the strength of beliefs about it act to preclude presentation of middle-ground positions and to tolerate procedural techniques of doubtful propriety. An example offered of the latter was allowing a numbered but textless amendment to be brought to the Senate floor before its sponsor was prepared to propose specific language.

While several pro-life participants were disposed to accept the analysis of congressional inability to resolve the abortion dispute and the assessment that usual congressional procedures and norms have not been violated, most of them rejected the idea that Congress should withdraw in favor of the courts. Symposium participants who favored continued legislative consideration of abortion insisted on the importance of legislative decision-making in a democracy. They did agree that the issue is "special" in importance and in the intensity of opinions about it. In their view, however, the preferred movement would be not to the courts, but directly to the floors of the House and Senate, and they believe their side to have been disadvantaged by inconsistency in the application of formal congressional rules.

Yet all sides acknowledge that Congress has acted on abortion many times. The present pro-choice majority has not shut out the minority. Indeed, the latter is transformed into a majority on the question of federal funding. There has been movement in committee and on the floor. No one knows how many committee hearings would be "enough," or how long floor debate should run, or just when a separate vote should be taken. What is clear is that hardly anyone cried "foul." Few complaints were made about trick plays. Congress has dealt with the abortion dispute in a messy and backdoor fashion, but neither side in the dispute claims to have been consistently shut off or shut out.

Presidential Appointments

According to Calvin Mackenzie's analysis, policy views have always been an appropriate and legitimate matter of concern in the selection and confirmation of presidential appointees. Just a few celebrated cases have recently provoked particular unease about the effects of the abortion dispute on the presidential appointment process. In fact, Mackenzie argued, the effects of the abortion issue to date have been neither broad nor deep. No nominee has been rejected by the Senate because of support for or opposition to abortion. The question did not even arise in confirmation proceedings until four years after the *Roe* decision. Nor is there evidence that any presidential nomination has been based solely on the abortion views of the nominee.

Still, Mackenzie read the challenges to the nominations of Justice Sandra O'Connor and Surgeon General C. Everett Koop in 1981 as possible harbingers of abortion's greater impact on the appointment process. Would such a development distort or threaten the system? One possible but unlikely effect could be stalemate between executive and legislature. A somewhat more plausible effect might be to inhibit the recruitment of good people who consider their abortion views to be private and are unwilling to discuss them.

To preclude trouble and keep the issue within proper bounds, Mackenzie proposed two "ground rules." First, pro-choice and pro-life activists should limit their involvement in the appointment process to those positions with jurisdiction over some aspect of abortion policy. Second, in those cases covered by the first rule, a nominee's views on abortion should not be the sole criterion by which suitability for appointment is judged.

Symposium participants of all persuasions tended to be less concerned about the fragility of the appointment process than did Mackenzie, less inclined than he to believe that jobs with jurisdiction over abortion policy could be separated from jobs without such jurisdiction, and more disposed to regard views on abortion policy as a proper subject of attention in any appointment and confirmation proceeding. The large number of participants espousing these positions did not do so out of an "everything-else-be-damned" mentality. Rather, they concluded that everything else would not be damned, that neither appointment nor confirmation is ever likely to turn on a person's attitude toward abortion, and that the legitimate benefits to either side from raising the issue far outweigh the costs to any nominee. It is widely understood, this argument continues, that in the last analysis the Senate does not allow substantive views to control confirmation decisions, that senators believe to do so would be to invite disaster. Not only has no nomination been lost because of abortion views, none is likely to be. Indeed, in the case of appointments to the federal bench, the point is virtually moot since nominees will inevitably avoid the problem by asserting the impropriety of ruling in advance and in the absence of a particular case.

Presidential appointees may quite properly be reminded by a confirmation fight that they will be under scrutiny and will be expected to act circumspectly. Pro-choice groups felt, for example, that their token opposition to the appointment of Joseph Califano, Jr., as secretary of health, education, and welfare in 1977 simply put the Carter administration on notice that it was being watched. Symposium participants readily agreed with the proposition advanced by one of them that activists need public devils. Groups challenging a nomination benefit from the visibility the challenge may accord them, from increased fund-raising opportunities, from spreading a nominee's past position on the record, and from the chance to extract limiting commitments from an otherwise antagonistic nominee. An illustration of the latter is Surgeon General Koop's commitment that if confirmed he intended to withdraw from the public battle over abortion policy. He was, and he did.

Participants agreed further that a president with strong ideological convictions should be expected to make appointments consistent with those convictions, but that an ideological position is not a sufficient condition to merit either appointment or confirmation. They also agreed that while abortion policy is not relevant to all presidential appointments, it is relevant in some way to many more appointments than might be assumed to be the case. While there are some differences between pro-life and pro-choice groups over which appointments fall within the relevant category, there is no disagreement over the right of each side to make up its own list.

Only a mild demurrer was entered to injecting the abortion issue into the appointment process in wholesale fashion rather than selectively. The objection turned on a belief that the wholesale approach may serve both groups of activists well and may not actually jeopardize nominees, but can put others in a difficult position. For example, if his nominees were regularly challenged over their abortion views without regard to the job and the general strength of the nominee, the president's ability to exercise broad discretion in appointments could be wiped out. Since that outcome would upset important institutional arrangements, self-restraint is not too much to ask or expect of activist groups. Participants again agreed that by and large there has been such self-restraint. No one suggested that any appointment battle yet fought should have been passed over. No one categorized any of the appointment battles yet fought as destructive.

The reaction of the symposium to Mackenzie's ground rules was that they are probably not needed. In this area, at least, symposium participants judged the abortion dispute to place established norms and institutions in even less jeopardy than did the essayist.

Public Opinion and Elections

What is public opinion on abortion policy? Can the single issue control electoral outcomes? Do elected representatives mirror the opinion of the electorate on the subject? According to Maris Vinovskis, methodological problems involving intensity of feeling, geographic distribution of respondents, and the ambivalence of many respondents are so formidable as to preclude confident judgments about public opinion, electoral behavior, and policy outcomes.

Public opinion on abortion may be murky, and analyzing it may be tricky, but the methodological problems need not be solved in order to evaluate some effects of the abortion dispute on the American political and electoral system. It is clear that pro-life and pro-choice groups each try to affect the outcomes of elections, that they each collect and spend money for that purpose, and that they sometimes fuse with other causes for ideological or strategic purposes and sometimes refuse all alliances. From all that is known, Vinovskis concludes that there is no cause to worry about a danger to the electoral system. Since symposium participants seemingly were persuaded that Vinovskis is correct on that score, they accepted his request to focus discussion on "fair" and "unfair" uses of money by pro-life and pro-choice political action groups.

The question underlying the symposium discussion was whether the respective electoral activities—especially those having to do with raising and spending money—are fair and reasonable enough to fall within the formal and informal rules governing American elections. That discussion revealed that each side perceives the electoral activity of its opposition to be different from its own, and that each believes its activity well within the usual norms. Indeed, each exhibited such intense self-approval of its own style as to imply disapproval of the ways of the opposition, although that disapproval was not made explicit.

Political action committees (PACs) abound for both pro-life and pro-choice positions. Pro-choice people believe financial support from their side represents fair and reasonable use because it is likely to go directly to candidates for office—more so, they assert, than is financial support that comes from pro-life PACs. But the pro-life people respond that while they may not spend a high percentage of their dollars directly on candidate support, they will spend those dollars on field personnel active in several campaigns. If that is so, the opposition responded, the costs should be allocated accordingly. So a dispute over whether pro-life money raised for one purpose is spent "fairly" for that purpose turned out to be as much a dispute over different ideas of neat accounting practices as over proper versus improper fund-raising techniques.

Pro-choice people "like to think," they say, that they spend money in electoral campaigns "more responsibly and more effectively" than do pro-life forces. By pro-choice accounts, they discourage emotional tactics; recruit and train for "responsible" electoral involvement; avoid pouring money into purely symbolic efforts; provide direct, positive support for candidates; and avoid the use of so-called hit lists—candidates targeted for attack. "We work to support our strongest defenders rather than to make examples out of opposition leaders," said one pro-choice activist, to the approval of her colleagues. The preferred technique is phone banks, not pickets. In fact, another went on, the goal is to mobilize as many people as possible to vote, not to terrorize candidates.

These methods of political involvement would all qualify as squarely in accord with normal practices. The pro-life side accepted without challenge most of the pro-choice description of its own side's behavior—doubting only that pro-choice has always avoided symbolic gestures of support in favor of channeling dollars to actual candidates in actual races.

Their own electoral style is different, explained the pro-life participants. Rather than folding into a larger cause, some pro-life PACs limit and target their expenditures to defeat vulnerable pro-choice candidates and elect pro-life candidates. "Whether it is called a hit list or called assessing priorities," said a pro-life activist, "it is rational to go after a candidate who won by a small margin rather than one who won by a large margin." The result may be a more impressive won-lost record—and one that is more frightening to opponents—than would otherwise be the case. Supporters of "negative expenditures" on the pro-life side said simply that they believe the technique works. They point to recent Senate votes to accept the Hyde amendment as evidence.

Not all pro-life PACs use the negative expenditures tactic. Some do not regard it as a practical way to advance their priorities, but none challenged its legitimacy. The pro-choice opposition denied the effectiveness of the technique, insisting that other factors account for particular electoral outcomes. It is significant that each side appeared disposed to take opposition tactics in stride. Neither said that unfair campaign tactics are used in an effort to influence abortion policy. The Jackson-Vinovskis judgment that there is no reliable estimate of the incidence of single-issue voters was unchallenged. The activists go about their business using electoral techniques with which they are comfortable and that they think are effective. But pro-life claims of success in particular instances meet countervailing claims by pro-choice people. Both sound confident.

When the pro-life and pro-choice electoral activists confronted each other, they were more disposed to explain the reasoning behind their respective electoral strategies than to suggest that strategies employed by the other side bend or exceed the understood rules of American politics. Virtually all of the activists participating in the symposium accept the proposition that on an issue as complex as abortion, it is virtually impossible to know the people's will separate from how legislators presumably reflect that will. Notwithstanding the impact on marginal races attributed to or claimed by activist groups, no election outcome can confidently be said to have turned solely or primarily on a candidate's pro-life or pro-choice views. Techniques used by the respective sides are not substantially different from those used by numerous other interest groups. In electoral politics, as in other areas explored in connection with the abortion dispute, there is less reason to be worried about distortion of the American system than some observers of the system may think to be the case. A divisive issue is not necessarily a destructive issue.

Symposium Participants

with their affiliations at the time of the symposium

Jodie T. Allen *The Washington Post*

David Beam *Senior Analyst, Advisory Commission on Intergovernmental Relations*

Wilfred R. Caron *General Counsel, United States Catholic Conference*

Cynthia Cates Colella *Analyst, Advisory Commission on Intergovernmental Relations*

Roger H. Davidson *Senior Specialist, American National Government and Public Administration, Congressional Research Service, U.S. Library of Congress*

Martha Derthick *Director, Governmental Studies Program, Brookings Institution*

Susan Dickler *Executive Director, Voters for Choice*

Nanette Falkenberg *Executive Director, National Abortion Rights Action League*

Lawrence M. Friedman *Marion Rice Kirkwood Professor of Law, Stanford Law School*

Patricia Gavett *Executive Director, Religious Coalition for Abortion Rights*

Peter Gemma *Executive Director, National Pro-Life Political Action Committee*

Oscar Harkavy *Chief Program Officer, Ford Foundation*

Cynthia E. Harrison *Deputy Director, Project '87 (sponsored by the American Political Science Association and the American Historical Association)*

A. E. Dick Howard *White Burkett Miller Professor of Law and Public Affairs, University of Virginia*

John E. Jackson *Professor of Political Science, University of Michigan*

Charles O. Jones *Professor of Political Science, University of Virginia*

Kenneth R. Kay *Chief Minority Counsel, Subcommittee on Separation of Powers, Senate Committee on the Judiciary*

G. Calvin Mackenzie *Associate Professor of Government, Colby College*

Judy Mann *The Washington Post*

Robert Marshall *Public Relations Director, American Life Lobby, Inc.*

Patrick McGuigan *Director, Judicial Reform Program, Free Congress Research and Education Foundation*

James C. Mohr *Professor of History, University of Maryland–Baltimore County*

Karen Mulhauser *Former Executive Director, National Abortion Rights Action League*

Burton Yale Pines *Vice President and Director of Research, Heritage Foundation*

Nelson W. Polsby *Visiting Scholar, Roosevelt Center for American Policy Studies*

A. James Reichley *Senior Fellow, Governmental Studies Program, Brookings Institution*

John Shattuck *Director, Washington Office, American Civil Liberties Union*

Gilbert Y. Steiner *Senior Fellow, Governmental Studies Program, Brookings Institution*

Susan Tolchin *Associate Professor of Public Administration, George Washington University*

Amy Vance *Program Officer, Human Rights and Governance, Ford Foundation*

Maris A. Vinovskis *Professor of History, University of Michigan*

Jane Wells-Schooley *Vice President–Action, National Organization for Women*

Cynthia E. Harrison

Appendix:
The Prohibition Experience

RATIFICATION of the Eighteenth Amendment in 1919 marked the first time in its history that the United States adopted an amendment to the Constitution that attempted to restrain the behavior of the citizenry, rather than that of the federal or state governments. The Constitution, which did not proscribe murder, trafficking in drugs, or armed robbery, now forbade the people to manufacture, sell, transport, import, or export "intoxicating liquors . . . for beverage purposes."

To implement the new provision, Congress quickly passed the National Prohibition Act. More commonly called the Volstead Act, the legislation represented the work of the general counsel of the Anti-Saloon League, the organization that had worked most devotedly for the Eighteenth Amendment's ratification. To the undoubted surprise of many, the Volstead Act adopted a stringent definition of "intoxicating liquors" that encompassed beer and wine. It also established a federal police force in the Bureau of Internal Revenue. Both the Volstead Act and the Eighteenth Amendment took effect January 16, 1920. Despite the severity of the law, prohibitionists expected few problems with enforcement. President Harding prophesied: "In another generation . . . liquor will have disappeared not merely from our politics, but from our memories." As the prestigious Wickersham Commission later noted, "It seems to have been anticipated that the fact of constitutional amendment and federal statute having put the federal government behind national prohibition would of itself operate largely to make the law effective."[1]

Funding decisions suggested that legislators did believe Prohibition

EDITOR'S NOTE: Scholars, activists, and politicians have claimed that enactment of a constitutional ban on abortion would create administrative and political problems analogous to those resulting from the constitutional ban on intoxicating liquors. A review of the Prohibition experience facilitates informed consideration of the validity and the limits of the analogy.

1. *Enforcement of the Prohibition Laws of the United States*, H. Doc. 722, 71 Cong. 3 sess. (Government Printing Office, 1931), p. 45.

would be easy to accomplish. Congress appropriated only $2.2 million the first year, although Senator Francis Warren asserted that the effort required $50 million. The Internal Revenue Bureau's budget provided for 1,500 Prohibition agents to police a nation 3 million miles square, with 105 million people, and a border of 18,700 miles. The states offered little assistance. Although forty-seven enacted "little Volstead Acts" detailing local regulations (only Maryland did not), they differed widely in their provisions, and the "concurrent power" that the amendment granted to the federal and state governments to enforce the law led to confusion. Moreover, in 1923 thirty states spent nothing to discharge their Prohibition laws and the remaining eighteen allocated only $550,000. Prohibitionists declined to press for more funding, fearing to imply that the law would be unpopular and difficult to enforce.

For the first two years, Prohibition seemed to bear out the positive predictions. Observers quickly noted the salubrious effects on the working classes: employers claimed "Blue Mondays" had disappeared, industrial accidents declined, arrests for public intoxication plummeted, public charities received fewer calls for assistance, and the divorce rate sank. In New York, alcohol-related deaths dropped from an average of more than 600 in 1916 and 1917 to 108 in 1921. In Boston, arrests for drunkenness dipped 55 percent and deaths from alcoholism were down 62 percent. Moreover, signs of increasing prosperity appeared across the nation. Industrial productivity rose, savings accounts grew, debt repayment improved. Prohibitionists without hesitation attributed these phenomena to the presence of the Eighteenth Amendment. Representatives of workers declined to accept this view. They suggested that these positive signs could more likely be attributed to better management, higher wages, and improved conditions of work.

Unanticipated Results

The first two years of the "noble experiment" proved to be largely a training period for those intending to defy the interdiction against liquor. Positive results were soon overwhelmed by ones less benign. Within a short time, professional criminals closed out small-time rumrunners with sophisticated networks involving massive shipments, extensive bribery of Prohibition agents, and a distribution system comprised of "blind pigs" (which pretended to sell only legal soft drinks, but in fact sold illegal potables) and covert speakeasies. As bootleggers became more familiar with methods to divert industrial alcohol, to acquire real beer secretly from breweries ostensibly producing only legal "near beer," to set up stills in private homes, and to market "moonshine," the abundance of intoxicating beverages in many cities reached or surpassed the pre-Prohibition level. By 1927–30, the per capita consumption of pure alcohol had climbed to 1.14 gallons per year, significantly higher than the 1921–22 average of 0.73 gallon, although still less than the 1.69 gallon average of 1911–14. Prohibition did bring about a change in the drinking population—as drinking acquired a cachet and necessitated higher expenditures, more consumers came from the middle class while many working-class beer devotees simply did without.

Other unanticipated results began to overcome the experiment. Prohibitionists had sought the new amendment as a device to shut down saloons. Before 1920, however, the saloons had at least been localized in downtown commercial areas. With the advent of the illegal still, establishments dispensing alcoholic beverages invaded residential areas. According to the *Detroit News*, there were 10,000 speakeasies in that city by 1923, compared to only 2,300 legal saloons in 1918.[2] The Wickersham Commission estimated in 1930 that 300,000 "speaks" dotted the nation, about twice as many drinking parlors as before the Prohibition movement had begun to close them down. New York City alone had some 32,000 undercover taverns by 1929, probably double the pre-Prohibition drinking places.

Senator Arthur Capper, among others, blamed incompetent and corrupt enforcement for the existence of such widespread disobedience. Not only had Congress and the states allocated too few funds to supply a sufficient number of agents, the Volstead Act exempted Prohibition investigators from the requirements of the civil service laws, a decision made at the request of the Anti-Saloon League, which wanted to ensure that sympathetic officers would be chosen. Ironically, this provision created a force comprised not of dedicated public servants but of political appointees of varying character, intelligence, and ability, often under the domination of local politicians who themselves had wavering commitments to the enforcement of the law. The citizenry was not impressed with these guardians of the legal system; the Wickersham Commission later commented: "To their reputation for general unfitness may be ascribed in large measure the public disfavor into which Prohibition fell."[3] The low pay these officers re-

2. Larry Engelmann, *Intemperance: The Lost War Against Liquor* (Free Press, 1979), p. 126. (Subsequent references to Prohibition experiences in Michigan are from this source.)

3. *Enforcement of the Prohibition Laws of the United States*, p. 12.

ceived, another effect of the unwillingness of the government to appropriate funds, made them ripe targets for bribery. Between January 1920 and June 1930, one agent in every twelve had been dismissed for cause, that is, some kind of malfeasance. Many of these men joined the illegal liquor network and put their expertise in enforcement operation to profitable use.

The problems with administration of the law existed at the top as well as at the bottom. Directors of Prohibition in the states quickly fell victim to the impossibility of implementing an unpopular law with inadequate resources. Between 1921 and 1925, 184 men held the 48 positions of state directors of Prohibition. New York City had four administrators of Prohibition within fourteen months. A pattern developed of sporadic, highly publicized crackdown campaigns, rather than a consistent, effective program.

Enforcement problems led proponents of the amendment to claim that the law had never had a fair trial, but public officials observed on many occasions that enforcement was virtually impossible, regardless of the amount of money allotted. The animus against the law in the cities was so strong that urban voters elected officials who openly promised to disregard the liquor laws. State and federal legislators themselves blatantly defied the law, and the public proved quite unperturbed about the matter. When a Prohibition officer raided a Republican banquet in Massachusetts and found his superior participating in the festivities, the agent, not his boss, lost his job.

The breadth of resistance to the law quickly overburdened the system designed to cope with it. Between January 1920 and June 1929 Prohibition agents seized more than a million and a half stills and fermenters and about 186 million gallons of spirits, beer, wine, and the materials to manufacture these products. They arrested more than half a million violators. Most cases did not require trials; even so, by 1925 almost 25,000 cases awaited disposition in the federal courts, an increase of almost 1,000 percent in five years. Although 62 percent of the arrests resulted in conviction, judges fearful of alienating communities that elected them issued mild penalties. In addition, to reduce the load on the courts, "bargain days" were established, during which violators would plead guilty and get off with a fine, rather than a jail sentence. After 1925, plea bargaining accounted for 91 percent of the convictions.

The crackdown enforcement campaigns not only burdened the judicial system; their excessive vigor often repelled the public. Newspapers carried frequent stories of armed agents shooting at bootleggers during their pursuit or drawing their guns to raid buildings thought to contain liquor. More than once innocent citizens were caught in the crossfire. By the end of the decade, over 1,000 civilians had been killed in the war against alcohol. Such punishment seemed too severe to suit the crime.

Similarly, another device to "protect" the public from illicit liquor provoked disgust from large segments of the populace. The Prohibition Bureau specified that manufacturers of industrial alcohol had to add denaturants to forestall diversion to the beverage market. Some additives merely tasted foul, but wood alcohol was both hard to detect and lethal. It was also substantially impossible to extract. Although the conscientious bootleggers did attempt to clean diverted industrial alcohol, thousands of people died every year from ingesting these poisons—an average of 4,000 annually between 1925 and 1930. Opponents argued that since the government knew that a percentage of industrial alcohol would be diverted to the underground beverage market, it should eliminate the use of toxic denaturants. The "drys" contended that the government had no responsibility to safeguard the lives of lawbreakers—an attitude that appeared to many as unacceptably callous.

If ordinary citizens were repelled by many aspects of enforcement and contemptuous of the law's goals, the underworld regarded the Eighteenth Amendment as a bonanza. Prohibition did not create the underworld network, but it provided an apparently bottomless source of income—much larger than that heretofore offered by prostitution and gambling. Citizens who would never dream of partaking of other activities run by professional criminals regarded drinking as a legitimate recreation. Moreover, middle-class businessmen patronizing bootleggers could hardly turn around and demand their arrest.

All of these unsavory consequences prompted concern about the impact of the Prohibition amendment on the traditional American respect for the Constitution, the law, and the legal system. Throughout the decade lawyers, legal scholars, government officials, jurists, and journalists warned that the contempt exhibited for the Eighteenth Amendment and its implementing regulations would have perilous consequences. As early as 1921 the Judicial Section of the American Bar Association maintained that leading citizens who violated this law were "aiding the cause of anarchy and promoting mob violence." In his inaugural address, President Hoover expressed a similar sentiment: "Our whole system of self-government will crumble either if officials elect what laws they will enforce or citizens elect what laws they will support. The worst evil of disregard for some law is that it destroys respect for all law."

In addition, Prohibition generated confusion about how to resolve conflict between the Eighteenth Amendment and other provisions of the Constitution, such as the protection against double jeopardy, the right to be free from unreasonable search and seizure, the autonomy of the states, and the separation between church and state. In general, the conflict was resolved in favor of execution of the Eighteenth Amendment. In 1922, for example, the Supreme Court decided (in *U.S.* v. *Lanza*) that defendants were not subjected to double jeopardy when tried for the same offense in both state and federal courts if the deed had simultaneously violated both state and federal laws. In another instance, in 1926 the Prohibition Bureau asked for the right to search private homes without warrants. Although Congress rejected this request, the Supreme Court appeared willing to expand this sphere of governmental activity, and in 1925 (*Carroll* v. *U.S.*) it affirmed the right of law enforcement officials to search private automobiles. In 1928 (*Olmstead* v. *U.S.*) it went further and approved the use of wiretapping evidence in a Prohibition case. Pushing the delicate balance between state and federal power to its limit, President Coolidge issued an order in May 1926 that state, county, and municipal officers could be federalized, a move criticized as a federal power grab and a derogation of states' rights. Some observers found too that with Prohibition the influence of the churches on politics had breached the barrier separating church and state. The Anti-Saloon League, with which more than 40,000 churches aligned themselves, received most of its funding from Protestant congregations and called itself "the church in action."

Political observers also voiced dismay over the effect of Prohibition on the political judgments of the populace. President Harding, finding his initial prophecy not borne out, told Congress in 1922 that the Eighteenth Amendment had not only failed to dispose of the issue, but rather intensified it so "that many voters are disposed to make all political decisions with reference to this single question." This type of political behavior, he warned, was "distracting the public mind and prejudicing the judgment of the electorate." George W. Norris, an abstainer and temperance advocate who served in the Senate from 1913 to 1943, later echoed both Harding's observation and his conclusion: "On both sides of this issue are prohibitionists supporting a prohibitionist, regardless of how he may stand on any other governmental question, and wet bigots, narrow-minded enough to support a man opposed to prohibition regardless of how he may stand on other questions. I am sorry that these things exist."

Yet another kind of complaint focused on the disregard of consensual boundaries of constitutional behavior on the part of law enforcement officials. Detroit's police commissioner justified warrantless raids on "blind pigs," which included the use of sledgehammers and axes, by contending that the law had to be broken to counter lawbreakers effectively. In New York City, Prohibition agents invited charges of entrapment when they established what came to be a popular speakeasy in order to entice bootleggers to offer their services.

Attempts at Improvement

Distress over the numerous unfortunate results of Prohibition finally led to the coalescence of antiprohibitionist sentiment in 1926, and the Association Against the Prohibition Amendment took up the fight for the modification of the Volstead Act. Although both pro- and antiprohibitionists agreed that the Eighteenth Amendment itself could not be repealed, reformers asserted that the legalization of beer and wine would eliminate most of the opposition to the amendment and would meliorate the disdain directed against the law. Notable citizens, like John D. Rockefeller, Jr., S. S. Kresge, and Alfred P. Sloan, who earlier had advocated Prohibition, supported modification, as did labor organizations and lawyers' groups.

Prohibitionists, for their part, instead tried to effect improved administration of the law. In March 1927 Congress reorganized the Prohibition enforcement structure and placed agents under the civil service rules. (Of the agents then employed, 59 percent failed the civil service test.) The outcome of the presidential election of 1928, which pitted a "wet" urban Irish Catholic, Al Smith, against a "dry" midwestern Protestant, Herbert Hoover, suggested that a majority of the population still favored the standard of abstinence. Convinced of popular backing and disturbed by the danger he saw in the continuing failure of Prohibition, President Hoover launched a reasonable effort to upgrade enforcement. He reformed many administrative procedures in the Federal Bureau of Investigation and the Prohibition Bureau, started the construction of five new federal prisons, streamlined judicial procedures, and appointed a prestigious Presidential Commission on Law Enforcement, known popularly by the name of its chairman, George W. Wickersham.

The Wickersham Commission produced several lengthy reports that clearly documented the failure of Prohibition, but the commission nevertheless recommended that the experiment be given one more try. Congress adopted the proposal to transfer the Prohibition Bureau from the Treasury to the Justice Department, and President Hoover promised to upgrade the bureau's personnel, to limit the use of firearms by its agents, and to concentrate enforcement on large-scale commercial enterprises.

The new effort had little impact. By the end of the decade illicit distilling, virtually impossible to thwart, had replaced either importation or diversion of industrial alcohol as the primary source of marketable liquor. Although the underground nature of the enterprise made accurate figures impossible to obtain, the Prohibition Bureau estimated that almost 900 million gallons of homemade intoxicating beverages found their way into the market. Congress still proved unwilling to allocate adequate funds for enforcement. In 1930 the Prohibition Bureau asked for $300 million and got $14 million. Nevertheless, prohibitionists refused to budge from their absolutist position. "Anything less than prohibition is permission," said the president of the New York Women's Christian Temperance Union.

The End of the Experiment

Depression suddenly changed the nature of the debate. With millions out of work, prohibitionists who had taken credit for the earlier prosperity now received opprobrium for the destruction of the national economy. Labor unionists argued that Prohibition had devastated not only the liquor industry, but ancillary enterprises as well, and asserted that the return of legal beer alone would employ a million men. With liquor legal and taxed, state and federal governments could restore their treasuries with dollars taken not from the law-abiding but from the pockets of criminals who sold intoxicants. Others pointed out that the demand for grain would provide a market for the troubled agricultural sector. By 1932 the Democratic platform supported outright repeal, and even the Republicans proposed reform —one "wet," the other "moist." The platforms reflected the majority of public sentiment. Between 1880 and 1919, voters in twenty-five state referenda were 56.3 percent dry; thirteen referenda held between 1930 and 1932 produced a 59.8 percent wet majority.

The 1932 election spelled the end of Prohibition, although the economy, not the liquor laws, constituted the determining factor in the Democrats' success. Within nine days of the new president's inauguration, Congress had passed a bill to legalize 3.2 percent beer. A repeal amendment cleared both houses of Congress in a mere eleven weeks and achieved ratification by convention—a procedure as close as possible to a national referendum and one that bypassed conservative, rural-dominated state legislatures— within ten months. Control of liquor manufacture and sale returned to the states; the great experiment was over.

The attempt to delimit the behavior of private citizens through constitutional amendment had failed. "We have somehow always contrived to have our prohibition, and our liquor, too," observed one law enforcement official. Nullification of the law through nonenforcement and disobedience with impunity created a situation in which liquor was plentiful, but unregulated. Without an overwhelming consensus on the desirability of abstinence, a constitutional amendment could not itself compel conformity without abrogating other, more important, principles—the sanctity of the home and person.

Whether a constitutional amendment proscribing abortion would be comparably futile is beyond the scope of this paper, as is speculation about the social consequences of such a policy measure. Drinking is not abortion, and the likely effects of a constitutional prohibition of the latter cannot be extrapolated in any simple way, if they can be extrapolated at all, from the historical experience of the former. It seems, nevertheless, desirable to be informed about the problems that developed in enforcing a constitutional restraint on personal behavior in the face of a large amount of public opposition.

In any event, the arguments on both sides of the abortion controversy do not rely heavily on assertions regarding the efficacy of a particular political course. Pro-life, as well as pro-choice, advocates are concerned above all with the values at stake in the decision. As in the case of Prohibition, the debate over a constitutional amendment limiting abortion centers finally on the signal issue: whose moral vision should the Constitution sustain?